EBURY P

RESILIENCE DECODED

A curious mind with a love for science and a gift for storytelling, Sujata Kelkar Shetty bridges cutting-edge research and everyday wellness with warmth and wisdom. Trained in the US as a biological scientist, she holds a BS in genetics (University of Wisconsin–Madison) and a PhD in toxicology (University of Kentucky), she then dived into pioneering stress research at the National Institutes of Health, Bethesda, Maryland, under Dr George Chrousos—a legend in the field. Her work revolves around decoding how stress tinkers with our immunity, one biomolecule at a time.

Back in India, she swapped lab coats for a pen, becoming a preventive health evangelist. For years, her lively columns in Mint (India's top business daily) made complex science feel like a friendly chat—mixing modern medicine, ancient ayurveda and real-world doctor insights. Readers loved it so much, she turned her wisdom into the bestselling book *99 Not Out! Your Guide to a Long and Healthy Life* (Penguin Random House India, 2019). The book was so popular that Penguin asked for an expanded edition which was published in 2023.

Sujata is also a certified life coach and resilience trainer on a mission to help people and organizations thrive. From Infosys to PricewaterhouseCoopers, her workshops crackle with energy, blending science, humour and practical tools to build unshakable well-being. She trained with Coaches Training Institute and Dr Amit Sood's Resilient Option.

When she's not writing or coaching, you'll find her reading, practising yoga or walking nature trails with her husband, two sons and three dogs. If the mood strikes, she will unwind with Hindustani classical music because even scientists need soulful melodies.

I0893588

ADVANCE PRAISE FOR THE BOOK

'This book is a labour of love, penned with clarity and empathy. Sujata brings both her professional training and her experience in raising two sons to bear on a topic that is top of mind across society today—teens in trouble. It is an invaluable resource for parents as well as teenagers'—**Rohini Nilekani, founder, Arghyam Foundation**

'A powerful guide to navigating life's challenges with courage and confidence, Sujata Kelkar Shetty equips teens and parents with the tools to build unshakable resilience and thrive'—**Rahul Dravid, former cricket player**

'Sujata Kelkar Shetty has created an essential road map for navigating the teen mental health crisis with both scientific precision and profound compassion. This book brilliantly combines cutting-edge neuroscience with practical strategies, offering parents the tools to raise resilient teenagers who can thrive despite unprecedented challenges'—**Dr Rajat Chauhan, sports and exercise medicine physician and founder of La Ultra - The High**

'A down-to-earth guide for tackling life's ups and downs with courage and confidence. Sujata Kelkar Shetty gives teens and parents practical tools to build real resilience and come out stronger'—**Sanjay Sharma, CEO, president and dean of the Asia School of Business, Kuala Lumpur, Malaysia**

'It speaks to parenting and pedagogical (yes, teachers would very much appreciate this book as well) challenges. The book provides a clear, pragmatic road map for any family trying to slay the "IB Dragon" and stay sane! In short, it is the essential handbook for any parent of adolescents'—**Jonathan Halden, principal of Ecolint, the International School of Geneva**

Resilience Decoded

What Every Parent Should Know About Teen Mental Health

Sujata Kelkar Shetty

EBURY PRESS
An imprint of Penguin Random House

EBURY PRESS

Ebury Press is an imprint of the Penguin Random House group of companies whose addresses can be found at global.penguinrandomhouse.com

Published by Penguin Random House India Pvt. Ltd
4th Floor, Capital Tower 1, MG Road,
Gurugram 122 002, Haryana, India

Penguin Random House India

First published in Ebury Press by Penguin Random House India 2025

Copyright © Sujata Kelkar Shetty 2025

All rights reserved

10 9 8 7 6 5 4 3 2

The views and opinions expressed in this book are the author's own and the facts are as reported by her which have been verified to the extent possible, and the publishers are not in any way liable for the same.

Please note that no part of this book may be used or reproduced in any manner for the purpose of training artificial intelligence technologies or systems.

ISBN 9780143476122

Typeset in RequiemText by Manipal Technologies Limited, Manipal
Printed at Gopsons Papers Pvt. Ltd., Noida

This book is sold subject to the condition that it shall not, by way of trade or otherwise, be lent, resold, hired out or otherwise circulated without the publisher's prior consent in any form of binding or cover other than that in which it is published and without a similar condition including this condition being imposed on the subsequent purchaser.

www.penguin.co.in

FSC www.fsc.org MIX Paper | Supporting responsible forestry FSC® C191020

To our sons Akash and Aarav

And a woman who held a babe against her bosom said, Speak to us of Children.

And he said:

Your children are not your children.

They are the sons and daughters of Life's longing for itself.

They come through you but not from you,

And though they are with you yet they belong not to you.

You may give them your love but not your thoughts,

For they have their own thoughts.

You may house their bodies but not their souls,

For their souls dwell in the house of tomorrow, which you cannot visit, not even in your dreams.

You may strive to be like them, but seek not to make them like you.

For life goes not backward nor tarries with yesterday.

You are the bows from which your children as living arrows are sent forth.

The archer sees the mark upon the path of the infinite, and He bends you with His might that His arrows may go swift and far.

Let your bending in the archer's hand be for gladness;

For even as He loves the arrow that flies, so He loves also the bow that is stable.

—Kahlil Gibran,
'On Children', from *The Prophet*

Contents

Foreword

In a world that demands more from our young people than ever before—academically, socially, emotionally—it has become imperative for parents, educators and mentors to understand not just what our teenagers are going through, but why. *Resilience Decoded* by Dr Sujata Kelkar Shetty arrives not a moment too soon. It is a clear, compassionate and deeply informed guidebook that speaks to every adult who cares about helping the next generation thrive in the face of increasing pressures.

Dr Shetty has done something remarkable. She's taken the complex science of the adolescent brain, layered it with wisdom from the worlds of psychology, parenting, education and sports, and rendered it into a book that is both enlightening and practical. Her voice is warm, honest and free of jargon. She doesn't preach or patronize—she partners with the reader, offering insight and support drawn from her work as a scientist, resilience coach, columnist and mother of two teenage boys.

What makes this book particularly valuable is its breadth. For parents, it offers not just understanding, but tools—ways to engage more meaningfully with your teen, model resilience yourself and build a home where emotional safety and mental strength go hand in hand. For schools, it provides context for student behaviour that is often misunderstood and misjudged. Dr Shetty shows how the teenage brain is uniquely capable, but still under construction—and how compassion, boundaries and consistent connection can create an environment where students flourish. And for sporting clubs, it offers essential lessons on how discipline, goal-setting, recovery and risk-taking interact with adolescent mental development—highlighting the role of coaches as powerful shapers of mindset, identity and resilience.

In all three spheres, the message is clear: resilience is not innate. It can be taught, modelled, nurtured and sustained. It is not about 'toughening up' or simply 'getting over it'. It's about helping young people develop the emotional, cognitive and behavioural skills to face challenges without being overwhelmed by them. And in today's climate—where mental health issues among youth are rising alarmingly—that message is not just important, it's urgent.

As someone who works closely with young people across diverse settings—from business mentoring to grassroots sports—I see the hunger for guidance daily. Adults want to help, but often don't know where to start. This book offers that starting point, and much more.

Dr Shetty's book is a road map. It is a source of both knowledge and hope. It reminds us that while we may not be able to remove every obstacle from our teenagers' paths, we can walk beside them—and help them build the internal strength to navigate whatever lies ahead.

I wholeheartedly recommend *Resilience Decoded* to every parent, teacher, coach and youth mentor. It is not just a book, it is a resource. It will shape the way you support the young people in your care.

—Greg Chappell

Preface

I am a mother of two teenage boys, navigating the beautiful chaos of adolescence in Bengaluru, India. My understanding of mental resilience was forged long before motherhood—in the laboratories of the National Institutes of Health in Bethesda, where I studied stress as a postdoctoral researcher, and in the quiet battlegrounds of my own mind, where I once wrestled with anxiety and its shadow, depression.

These twin spectres first visited me during my PhD years in the US, when the weight of isolation and unrelenting pressure dulled the vibrancy of life. Back then, I mistook my suffering for mere fatigue—an inevitable tax of ambition. It wasn't. The second reckoning came with motherhood, a time that should have been luminous but was instead clouded by upheaval: a transcontinental move, new cities (Washington to Delhi to Mumbai to Bengaluru in two dizzying years) and the seismic shift into parenthood. Stress, I learned, is a cunning architect—it builds its labyrinth fastest in those genetically predisposed. And, without the scaffolding of social support, escape feels impossible.

The second time around, I fought back—armed with therapy, science and an unshakable resolve to reclaim my mind. I immersed myself in the study of resilience, weaving research into my monthly column, *Wellness Sutra*, for *Mint Business*. Writing was therapeutic, transmuting pain into purpose. I rebuilt myself through long walks in Cubbon Park and ashtanga yoga, through magnesium and B12, and through the radical act of guarding sleep like a sacred covenant. Gluten, I discovered, was a stealthy saboteur; its exile banished years of migraines. Slowly, life regained its texture—music, laughter, the ordinary magic of existing without dread.

This hard-won equilibrium led me to resilience coaching, then to my first book, *99 Not Out!* (Penguin Random House India, 2019), and now here—to this book, born of equal parts urgency and love. Because I know what it is to be young and faltering, to lack the tools to weather inner storms. And because I am now the mother of teenagers, watching as they navigate a world that demands too much, too soon.

Like all parents, I once naively assumed each stage would grow easier—only to learn, as my wise grand-aunt warned, that the responsibility of motherhood expands with their height. Adolescence is a tightrope between fragility and brilliance; their brains are works in progress, their emotions raw wiring. The data is unequivocal: today's teens face a mental health epidemic, with anxiety and depression surging like silent tsunamis. The reasons are etched in their biology—a tempest of neurodevelopmental change, hormonal surges and social crucibles—yet our systems still treat them as 'little adults', ill-equipped to address their unique needs.

This book is my answer. A synthesis of interviews with psychologists, educators and teens themselves combined with cutting-edge research and hard-earned personal truths. It is for parents who lie awake wondering how to armour their children against invisible battles. My husband and I cling to the finite years before our sons leave for college, stealing hugs from their resistant shoulders, whispering *you are enough* into the roar of achievement culture. We fail often. But we persist—because resilience is not inherited, it is modelled.

The stakes couldn't be higher. This generation's well-being demands a dual mandate: healing those already wounded, and equipping the healthy with unshakable coping armour. Let this book be your compass in that mission.

Now—let's begin.

Introduction

India announced an unprecedented nationwide lockdown in March 2020 to contain the spread of COVID-19. Extended multiple times, it confined children to their homes for two mind-numbing academic years. Schools and colleges remained largely shuttered throughout this period, bringing exhaustion, frustration and boredom for parents and children alike. Families grappled with the monotony of life indoors, strained relationships from lack of personal space and the financial hardships wrought by the pandemic. Lockdowns and remote learning also severed vital in-person connections with classmates, friends and teachers—a blow that hit India's teen mental health especially hard. In this book, 'teenagers' and 'adolescents' refer to youth aged 11 to 19 and I use these terms interchangeably.

Research from the pandemic era reveals that abrupt disruptions to academic routines—particularly school closures—likely contributed to rising anxiety among older adolescents.[1] In India, nearly 32 crore students faced uncertainty about education and career prospects. While comprehensive data on the psychological toll remains scarce, existing studies confirm that teen mental health deteriorated during the pandemic, with effects lingering long after.[2] Therapists in Delhi, Mumbai and Bengaluru reported practices 'bursting at the seams', with waitlists stretching months.

For two years, teens lived online. The toxic interplay of social isolation and social media—a pandemic lifeline for many—worsened their struggles. A University of California, Davis study found that shuttered classrooms led to heightened stress, diminished social inclusion and plummeting school satisfaction.[3] Teens in online programmes showed significantly higher rates of depression and anxiety than their in-person peers. This disparity was measurable because, unlike India's blanket two-year school closures, the US allowed regional variability.

An Indian study found that one in four teens experienced severe or extreme depression and anxiety, while one in three reported mild-to-moderate symptoms.[4] Though the pandemic has ended, these numbers show no signs of rapid decline. Psychologists nationwide observe this trend, echoed by US research: while adult mental health rebounded to pre-pandemic levels, adolescents continue to battle anxiety and depression.[5]

Stress: A Double-Edged Sword

Conventional wisdom treats stress as an unqualified evil—to be avoided at all costs. But this 'stress avoidance' mindset overlooks its necessity. Moderate stress is not just normal; it's essential for growth. Teens must master complex social and intellectual skills to transition into adulthood. This process is inherently stressful, yet vital. Demonizing all stress risks pushing adolescents to disengage from healthy challenges—rigorous academics, athletics or creative pursuits—ultimately handicapping their futures.

The pandemic, however, unleashed a tsunami of toxic stress: social isolation, existential uncertainty, job losses, and for many, the trauma of losing parents. While some stress builds resilience, chronic overwhelm can break even adults, let alone vulnerable teens. To shield them from long-term harm and prepare them for a competitive world, we must teach them to navigate challenges, not flee them. Resilience—a lifelong asset—enables this.

The Path to Healing

Anxiety and depression often resolve with time, sometimes requiring only a listening ear. Yet there's a sobering caveat: when these conditions take root in adolescence, the risk of recurrence in adulthood rises. This makes early intervention critical.

Today's teens face a perfect storm. They've weathered a pandemic, confront climate doom and are bombarded with warnings that AI may erase their career prospects—all while navigating hormonal changes, academic pressure and parental expectations. Globally, 20 per cent of adolescents grapple with mental health issues yearly. Depression and anxiety rank among the top causes of disability in this age group.

Why do so many suffer untreated? Ignorance and stigma play starring roles. Parents, teachers and even healthcare workers often miss the signs. Some teens beg for therapy, only to be dismissed by parents who insist 'nothing's wrong'. Others face refusal to fund treatment. This denial stems partly from cultural taboos—mental health remains shrouded in secrecy in Indian households—and partly from generational disconnect.

'Teens today have more comforts and opportunities than we did,' one parent remarked. But material ease doesn't guarantee emotional security. In our hypercompetitive world, we must ask: Are we pushing too hard? Helicopter parenting—micromanaging lives to eliminate struggle—backfires spectacularly. Studies confirm that overprotected children develop poorer mental health.[6] Yet 'time-intensive parenting' is now a global norm, with Indian, American and British parents spending unprecedented hours directing homework, hobbies and social lives. I, too, am a recovering helicopter parent.

Resilience Through Adversity

Resilience isn't innate; it's forged by overcoming challenges. Research shows that adults who faced measured adversity in youth rebound better from setbacks. By shielding teens from every failure, we rob them of resilience. As the adage goes: How will they learn to rise if they never fall?

The world we grew up in no longer exists. Today's teens inherit a planet on the brink—environmentally, politically and economically. Add social media's distortions, academic grind and parental pressure, and their despair becomes understandable.

How This Book Helps

This book is a roadmap for parents navigating their teen's mental health. It blends science with practical strategies, acknowledging India's unique cultural barriers—stigma, privacy concerns and the myth that struggle is shameful.

Chapter 1 explores the teenage brain: a powerhouse for learning but prone to reckless choices due to immature decision-making circuits.

Chapter 2 details resilience-building habits—movement, nutrition, sleep and creative expression—to prevent mental health crises.

Chapter 3 decodes social media's pitfalls, from cyberbullying to unqualified 'influencer' advice.

Chapter 4 guides parents in balancing support with independence, plus self-care to avoid burnout.

Mental health medication has its place, but this book emphasizes minimal medical intervention wherever possible. And asks parents to focus instead on behavioural and environmental fixes. Yet it also challenges parents to model resilience themselves—because teens learn more from our actions than our advice.

This book is written as a resource for parents who want to understand and nurture their teens and their mental health better. It is also a resilience guide to help prevent the mental health black holes that so many of our young people are falling into. And finally, this book serves to support parents and caregivers in looking after their own well-being as they tirelessly work to support their families and their community.

Ultimately, this is a call to arms: to raise a generation that doesn't just survive life's waves, but learns to ride them.

Key Takeaways: Introduction

- The pandemic has intensified mental health issues among teenagers, with rising rates of anxiety and depression.
- Social media, isolation and academic pressures have deepened teen vulnerabilities.
- Resilience is not innate—it can be compassionately taught, practiced and reinforced.
- Parents must address both healing (for those struggling) and strengthening (for those not yet in crisis).
- Prevention through lifestyle, connection and emotional intelligence is as vital as professional intervention.

1

The Ferrari Brain

Among all human organs, the brain takes the longest to develop. At birth, it's only 40 per cent of its eventual adult size. As we grow, our brains don't just expand in volume—they undergo continuous rewiring of their internal connections.

During adolescence, the brain reaches full physical size but remains structurally incomplete. It contains an overabundance of grey matter (the neurons forming the brain's building blocks) but relatively little white matter (the nerve fibres enabling efficient communication between brain regions). Frances E. Jensen and Amy Ellis Nutt perfectly capture this in *The Teenage Brain: A Neuroscientist's Survival Guide to Raising Adolescents and Young Adults*, comparing the adolescent brain to 'a brand new Ferrari—primed and pumped but not yet road tested.'

This biological reality creates a fundamental tension in how we perceive and treat teenagers. Their adult-like physical appearance often leads us to expect adult-like behaviour and judgment. However, we must recognize that teenage brains remain far from fully developed. Their brains literally shape themselves through environmental cues and experiences—meaning every interaction and lesson we provide directly influences their neurological development and future capabilities.

Structurally, our brain sits on the brain stem which connects it with the spinal cord. Neuroscientists divide the brain into four sections or lobes: the frontal, parietal, temporal and the occipital. The back of the brain houses the cerebellum. The cerebellum regulates our motor function, or the movement and coordination of our limbs. The occipital lobe is where our visual cortex, responsible for our vision, is housed. The parietal lobes are where our senses of touch, smell, taste and hearing reside, among other things. The temporal lobe is where our ability to manage our feelings, our sexuality and our language reside. The frontal lobe is where executive functioning, judgement, insight and impulse control are housed. It is also the part of the brain that is responsible for planning, problem solving and assessing risk and danger. In other words, when we decide on which course of action to take, this is the area of the brain that helps us make that decision with wisdom. The frontal lobes are responsible for what puts us on top of the food chain in the animal kingdom. They give us the competitive edge but like all good things, we have to wait for our brains to metamorphose into their elegant adult versions.

Adolescence is a period of intense change for the human brain. The brain goes through a transformation and this transformation is associated with what infuriates us about our teens and some other incredible qualities as well. Our teens have the capacity for remarkable courage, risk-taking and creative expression. While the brain stops growing in size in early adolescence, the teen years are all about fine-tuning the inner machinery of how the brain works. The brain only finishes developing and maturing in the mid-to-late twenties. When I told my sons that I would treat them as fully functioning adults only after they had crossed their mid-20s, they rolled their eyes!

The part of the brain behind the forehead, called the prefrontal cortex, is one of the last parts of the brain to mature. This area is responsible for skills like planning, prioritizing and making good decisions. Because the frontal lobes are still developing, teenagers rely—more than adults do—on a part of the brain called the amygdala to make decisions and solve problems. The amygdala is the part of the brain that generates emotions, impulses, aggression and instinctive behaviour. Emotions generated here from sub-cortical areas wash over the cortical circuits of reasoning. The downsides are emotional storms and moodiness, and sub-optimal and often impulsive decision-making—the behaviours that we parents find exasperating in our teens! This emotion-driven reasoning is also why adolescents push against the status quo. The upside of the amygdala being in charge is a powerful passion to live life fully and the ability to create new things and make interesting connections and discoveries. These are qualities we all want our teens to integrate into their personalities so that they grow into the kind of adults they are meant to be—adults who lead creative, fulfilling and engaged lives. Adults who contribute to the world in meaningful and important ways.

One of the other things that is unique to the teen brain is that it is more sensitive to dopamine, a neurotransmitter made in the brain. Dopamine plays a crucial role in the brain's reward centre, what neuroscientists like to call the mesolimbic pathway. It plays a starring role in pleasure, motivation and learning. It is our 'happy' neurotransmitter—the more dopamine we have circulating in our brains, the happier we are. As humans, our brains are hard-wired to seek out behaviours that release dopamine in our reward centre. When you're doing something pleasurable, your brain releases a large amount of dopamine. You feel good and you seek more of that feeling. This is why junk food and sugar are so addictive—they trigger the release of a large amount of dopamine into your brain.

There is a shift in the brain's dopamine system during adolescence—there is a growth of dopamine transmitters and an enhanced supply of dopamine in the brain. What that means for teens is that they get far greater pleasure than adults when they engage in an activity like sex, for example. Because of this same heightened sensitivity to dopamine, teens tend to pursue new experiences that give them that dopamine surge, associated with intense emotion. This is where their love for risk-taking and thrill-seeking comes in. As parents, we are all well aware of the downsides of teenage novelty-seeking, but we sometimes forget the upside. Novelty-seeking gives our teens the courage to leave their familiar environment and the safety of home for the unfamiliar and potentially unsafe world beyond. Thrill-seeking during these years gives our teens something to enjoy as they navigate the overwhelming task of growing up.

The teen brain then is uniquely able and has an amazing ability to adapt and respond to new experiences and situations. Whether it is by taking challenging classes, exercising or engaging in creative activities like art or music, all these can strengthen brain circuits and help the brain mature. Yet, teen brains are also extremely vulnerable. If you have ever wondered why your teen can win debates on current events with you in one moment while seeming impulsive or irrational in another, this is why. The back-to-front development of the brain and the distinct changes in how its reward centre operates explain these shifts and changes.

Our teenagers are working with brains that are still under construction. Teenagers do not lack intelligence—they navigate life with brilliance. What they lack is the neurological scaffolding to harness their brilliance consistently. Now that you are armed with this knowledge, those exasperating 'teen' moments will be easier to bear!

Brain Basics

Frances E. Jensen and Amy Ellis Nutt write in *The Teenage Brain* that among all the organs of the human body, the brain takes the longest to develop. At birth, it is only 40 per cent of the size it will be in adulthood. Not only does the brain grow in size, it also changes in its internal wiring as it develops. By adolescence, while the brain has reached its full size, the structure is yet far from complete. There is an overabundance of grey matter, or the neurons that form the building blocks of the brain, with a limited supply of white matter, the nerve fibres that serve to help information flow efficiently from one part of the brain to the other. Therein lies the problem for teenagers and how they are perceived. Because they physically look like adults, we start treating them like adults. But it is crucial that we understand that teen brains are far from ready for the real world in the way that adult brains are. The teen brain gets ready for the real world based on the cues and stimuli that are present during its development, changing the way that it functions later in life.

Structurally, our brain sits on the brain stem which connects it with the spinal cord. The brain itself is divided into four sections or lobes: the frontal, parietal, temporal and the occipital. The back of the brain houses the cerebellum. The cerebellum regulates our motor function, or the movement and coordination of our limbs. The occipital lobe is where our visual cortex, responsible for our vision, is housed. The parietal lobes are where our sensory cortex resides, among other things. The temporal lobe is where emotional regulation, sexuality and language reside. The frontal lobe is where executive function, judgement, insight and impulse control reside. Since the brain matures from the back to the front, in the teen years the frontal lobes are the least mature and connected as compared with the other lobes.

The frontal lobes are where we generate insight and judgement. It is also the part of the brain that is responsible for planning, problem solving and assessing risk and danger. In other words, when we decide on which course of action to take, this is the area of the brain that helps us make that decision with wisdom. Taken together, the frontal lobes are responsible for what makes us uniquely human adults. They give us the competitive edge in the animal kingdom but also take a long time to connect and mature.

The National Institutes of Health (NIH) conducted a major study to see how brain areas activate and mature over the first twenty-one years of life and they found that brain connectivity works its way from the back to the front.[1,2] So that the last place to connect is the frontal lobe. The teen brain is only 80 per cent mature and the last 20 per cent of the maturity that is remaining in the frontal lobes explains the irrational behaviour of our teens—the impulsiveness, the inability to follow through, the inability to focus and the temptation to engage in risky activities. Our teens will grow into rational and intelligent adults one day, but they aren't there yet, because that's just how the human brain develops.

How then can we lovingly support our teens with their brain vulnerabilities? By sharing real life stories and their real life consequences with them over and over again. At dinner, during school pick up, when they are grabbing a snack and you a coffee, even when they complain that they've heard it before, which they will. The reason that you need to repeat yourself is again based on what we know about brain development. The ability to hold in your mind that a certain task needs to be done in the future—like returning a phone call or finishing a school-related task—isn't quite developed during the teen years. This ability, called prospective memory, starts to strengthen in our childhood and then again in our twenties. In our teen years, however, when there is quite a lot to juggle, our prospective memory doesn't improve, so our support in managing task completion is needed.

Multitasking, something many teens claim to do well, is extremely challenging for our teenagers. Switching between tasks depends on the parietal lobes which are responsible for association and aren't fully developed in teens. So while they may pride themselves for being able to multitask, they actually can't. When the brain has to focus and engage in multiple activities like talking on the cell phone and driving, it has to constantly switch back and forth and neither activity gets done particularly well. This is true for adults too, but is particularly true in teens. In the US, of the nearly six thousand teens who die in car accidents, a whopping 87 per cent die because they were driving when distracted.[3]

One of the other things that is unique to the teen brain is that it is more sensitive to dopamine, a neurotransmitter made in the brain. Dopamine plays a crucial role in the brain's reward centre, what neuroscientists like to call the mesolimbic pathway. It plays a starring role in pleasure, motivation and learning. It is our 'happy' neurotransmitter—the more dopamine we have circulating in our brains, the happier we are. As humans, our brains are hard-wired to seek out behaviours that release dopamine in our reward centre. When you're doing something pleasurable, your brain releases a large amount of dopamine. You feel good and you seek more of that feeling.

This is why junk food and sugar are so addictive. They trigger the release of a large amount of dopamine into your brain.

A study on distracted driving in India published by SaveLIFE Foundation uncovered that 47 per cent of people receive calls on their mobile phone while driving and 60 per cent of the people who receive calls while driving don't stop at a safe location to take the call. It would come as no surprise then that the study also found that India has the highest number of road crash fatalities, with a crash occurring every minute and one death every four minutes. And it's a sobering fact indeed to know that our country has just 1 per cent of the world's vehicles, but accounts for over 10 per cent of global road crash fatalities.[4] While we know that most of these drivers in India are probably adults, distracted driving would certainly play a major role in teen driver-related accidents too.

Multitasking is also bad for their studies as it profoundly affects a teen's ability to memorize and retrieve information. Researchers at the University of Missouri studied how multitasking affects the ability of teenagers to memorize words and retrieve them late.[5] They found that if a distracting task was present while teens were trying to memorize something, their ability to memorize dropped on average by about 50 per cent.

General Tips for Helping Teens with Their 'Ferrari' Brains

1. **Reinforce Lessons Through Repetition**

   Share real-life stories with real consequences repeatedly—until they remind you at least twice they've heard them before! This repetition helps their developing brains strengthen cause-and-effect connections, gradually wiring these patterns into their thinking.

2. **Model Single-Tasking**

   Lead by example in reducing multitasking. Explain that:
   - Task-switching is especially challenging for developing teen brains.
   - Even adults become less efficient when multitasking.
   - Focused attention yields better results in school and daily life.

3. **Create a Balanced Home Environment**

   Combine warmth with structure to provide optimal support:
   - Express love frequently through words and actions.
   - Maintain clear, safety-oriented rules.
   - Help them present their best self to the world.

4. **Highlight Their Resilience**

   Teens often struggle to see beyond immediate challenges. Help them recognize their capabilities by:

- Reminding them of past difficulties they successfully overcame.
- Pointing out how previous 'disasters' often work out positively.
- Emphasizing their growing problem-solving skills.

5. **Engage With Their Interests**

   Show genuine curiosity about their world (even if you don't share their taste in hip-hop!):

   - Ask questions about their hobbies and passions.
   - Recognize that valuing their interests is equal to valuing them.

6. **Ask Before Advising**

   When they share problems, check first:

   - 'Would you like my thoughts, or just need me to listen?'
   - Most often, they simply want your attentive silence—the gift of being heard without judgment.

Genius Level Tips

1. **Strategic Story Reinforcement**

   Share real-life stories *with a twist*:

   - First tell the story straight.
   - Next time, ask *them* to predict the consequences.
   - Finally, have them retell it to a younger sibling

   Pro Tip: This 'teach-back' method boosts retention by 50 per cent.[6]

2. **The Single-Tasking Challenge**

   Turn focus into a game:

   - Create a family 'deep work hour' with phones in baskets.
   - Offer bonus screen time for every uninterrupted homework session.
   - Show them your own work calendar with blocked focus periods.

   Neuroscience Hack: The brain releases dopamine when completing singular tasks, creating natural rewards.

3. **Balanced Home Lab**

   Build an environment that subconsciously trains executive function:

   - Install whiteboards for goal-tracking (visible means actionable).
   - Use color-coded calendars for family schedules.
   - Implement 'question hours' when all non-urgent queries wait.

   Design Insight: Environmental cues reduce 40 per cent of parent-teen conflicts.

4. **The 5-Minute Rule**

   Before problem-solving discussions:

   - Set a timer for pure listening

- Then ask: 'Would you like my a) Experience b) Advice c) Just empathy?'

Communication Breakthrough: Teens given choice in support style engage with their parents longer.

The Transformative Teenage Brain: A Learning Powerhouse

The adolescent brain undergoes extraordinary changes that unlock unprecedented learning potential. Research confirms this period represents a golden window for cognitive development—teen brains are biologically primed to absorb, analyse and master complex skills like never before.[7]

The brain enters a new world of abstract thinking where between the ages of 14–18 and beyond, neural circuits are strengthened enabling the following capacities in our teens:[8]

- **Advanced reasoning**: The ability to grasp abstract concepts like justice, democracy and evolution.
- **Systems thinking**: The ability to understand interconnected systems like geometry, government and biological processes.
- **Nuanced analysis**: The ability to differentiate evidence from opinion, weighing multiple causal factors.

- **Emotional complexity**: The ability to recognize mixed emotions and social contradictions (e.g., curated social media happiness vs reality).

As abstract thinking develops, teens gain remarkable control over their own learning:[9]

- They start to recognize how emotions impact focus.
- They can develop strategies to manage distractions.
- They can learn to inhibit unproductive thoughts.
- They start to appreciate diverse viewpoints as valuable knowledge sources

The Emotional Advantage

Contrary to stereotypes:

- Most teen emotional swings are *positive*—characterized by excitement, optimism and idealism.
- These emotional intensities become powerful drivers of curiosity and engagement.
- The brain's heightened plasticity makes memories formed during adolescence more durable.

IQ: The Surprising Truth

Groundbreaking research overturns old assumptions.[10,11]

- ~33 per cent maintain stable IQ scores through adolescence.
- ~33 per cent show significant IQ *increases* (linked to resilience-building and sustained motivation).
- ~33 per cent experience declines (often tied to environmental factors).

Critical Window for Skill-Building

This period demands focused development of:

1. **Learning strategies**: Structured review plans, self-testing techniques, progress reflection.
2. **Talent cultivation**: Identifying and nurturing innate strengths.
3. **Targeted support**: Addressing learning challenges or mental health needs promptly.

Key Insight: This isn't merely preparation for adulthood—it's a unique biological state where the brain operates at peak learning capacity. The practical strategies that follow will help maximize this irreplaceable developmental phase.

Science-Backed Strategies to Boost Your Teen's Learning

1. **The Power of Handwritten Notes**[12]

   Why it works:

   - Deepens neural processing compared to typing.
   - 70 per cent better retention when paraphrasing vs copying.

   Pro Tip: Encourage color-coding key concepts for visual reinforcement.

2. **Master Mind Mapping**

   The visual advantage:

   - Our brains process visuals 60,000x faster than text.[13]
   - Creates 'mental hooks' for recalling interconnected ideas.

   Try this: Use apps like Miro or old-school coloured pens for creative mapping.

3. **Read Aloud for Stronger Recall**

   The production effect:

   - Speaking text activates 3x more brain regions than silent reading.
   - Particularly effective for memorizing formulas, dates, and vocabulary.

Bonus: Recording and replaying audio notes doubles retention.

4. **The Spaced Learning Method**

   Beat the forgetting curve:

   - tudy the material, wait 2–3 days, review and identify gaps while focusing only on weak areas.

   Science says: Spaced repetition improves recall by 200 per cent.[14]

5. **Sleep for Memory Consolidation**

   The magic happens at night:

   - During deep sleep, the brain replays and stores daily learning.
   - Just thirty minutes more sleep improves test performance by 15 per cent.

   Key: Maintain consistent sleep schedule even on weekends.

6. **Strategic Planning Beats Cramming**

   'The 3-2-1 Study Plan':

   - 3 weeks before tests: Begin light review
   - 2 weeks out: Daily focused sessions
   - 1 week prior: Practice tests under timed conditions

   Parent role: Help break big projects into weekly milestones.

7. **Curate Quality Learning Resources**

Be a learning detective:

- Identify reliable YouTube educators (e.g., CrashCourse, Khan Academy).
- Build a reference library with varied formats (books, podcasts, documentaries).

Remember: Guide them to resources rather than providing answers.

8. **The Digital Detox Challenge**

Why it matters:

- Just having a smartphone nearby reduces focus by 20 per cent.[15]

Solution: Implement 'focus hours' with all devices in another room.

Compromise: Allow music without lyrics during study sessions.

9. **Emotional Regulation Toolkit**

For parents during meltdowns:

- The 4-7-8 breathing method (inhale for 4 seconds, hold 7, exhale 8).

Script: 'I see this is frustrating. Let's pause and revisit in 20 minutes.'

Science-backed: Co-regulation helps teens develop self-control.

Adolescents show greater attraction to risk and uncertainty compared to both children and adults—a developmentally beneficial trait we'll explore in detail next.

Risk-Taking

Risk-taking—behaviour with uncertain outcomes—is fundamentally woven into the teenage experience. As adolescents navigate increasing responsibilities while facing pivotal life choices, their natural appetite for risk can unsettle even the most composed parents. Evolutionarily, this makes perfect sense. The tolerance for uncertainty that characterizes adolescence serves crucial developmental purposes, enabling young people to separate from familial safety nets and establish their independence. Whether attempting new skills, running for student government or standing up for friends, these 'first-time' experiences feel particularly risky precisely because they are firsts. This willingness to approach the unknown with curiosity represents an essential adaptive quality—one that will later empower them to live as autonomous adults.

However, the teenage brain's unfinished development creates a paradox. The underdeveloped frontal lobes impair accurate danger assessment, particularly regarding high-stakes risks like unprotected sex or substance use. While evolution may favour risk-taking as adaptive in the long term, the immediate dangers remain all too real—explaining many parental sleepless nights.

Contemporary adolescence presents unprecedented risk landscapes. Today's teens navigate a world where potential dangers—from unfiltered internet access to globalized peer influences—dwarf those faced by previous generations. Centuries ago, community oversight and limited mobility naturally constrained risky behaviours. Modern teens, by contrast, confront both expanded opportunities and exponentially more dangerous temptations, all while being particularly susceptible to social suggestion—whether from peers in the next room or influencers across the globe.

The social dimension of risk-taking reveals another complexity. Research shows teens take more risks when peers are present—not necessarily due to direct pressure, but because shared experiences amplify reward sensations.[16] While we often focus on peer-enabled negative risks, friends equally encourage positive risks: defending beliefs, volunteering or standing against bullying. These beneficial risks foster growth in ways that safe choices cannot.

Neurochemically, dopamine drives adolescent risk-taking. This 'feel-good' neurotransmitter floods teen brains more intensely than child or adult brains during novel experiences—regardless of eventual outcomes.[17] This heightened sensitivity means teens aren't irrational; their reasoning abilities near adult levels by mid-adolescence. Rather, their brains simply assign greater reward value to new experiences. When risky behaviour yields no immediate consequences, the dopamine surge creates powerful reinforcement—making prevention more effective than remediation.

This neurodevelopmental reality presents both a challenge and an opportunity. While we must maintain open dialogues about irreversible consequences, we should equally encourage positive risks: leadership roles, new activities, social courage.[18]

The art of parenting adolescents lies in channelling their natural risk-taking impulses toward growth while safeguarding against genuine dangers—a balancing act as old as humanity itself, yet newly complex in our digital age.

The Dual Nature of Teen Risk-Taking

Teenagers' propensity for risk-taking then represents both a challenge and an opportunity. While this tendency can lead to dangerous choices with potentially irreversible consequences, it also fuels growth and achievement when channelled positively. Our role then is to act as guides where we discuss the real-world impact of risky decisions while paralleling encouraging constructive risk taking such as:

- Leadership roles (student government)
- New extracurricular activities (debate, theatre)
- Social courage (making new friends, standing against bullying)

A Young Entrepreneur's Perspective

Shreyank Hebbar, 22-year-old co-founder of SustainGuard Technologies, outdoor enthusiast, and self-proclaimed foodie, reflects on his teenage risk-taking:

> *As a teenager, I was far from a model student. I got into trouble at school more times than I can count, even getting suspended on several occasions because of risky behaviours. Poor grades and constant trips to the principal's office became a regular part of my life, much to my parents' frustration. My parents were concerned but never overly strict. They didn't force me to change but instead tried to make me understand the consequences of my actions, all while giving me the freedom to make my own decisions and learn from life. That freedom, though it led to some mistakes, ultimately helped me grow.*

Looking back, I realize I just needed to figure things out on my own. As I got older, I began to realize what I wanted out of life, and with that came more discipline. Now, I'm more confident, driven, and ambitious, and I owe a lot of that to the lessons I learnt from my rebellious years. I learned perseverance through failure and gained the independence I needed to push forward.

Today, my relationship with my parents is stronger than ever. We have a loving bond, and they're proud of me no matter what. It's proof that even if you don't always follow the straight path, you can still end up where you're meant to be when you have supportive parents who guide you without trying to control you.

Guiding Teens to Channel Their Risk-Taking Instincts Wisely

1. **Build Trust Through Early, Open Communication**
    - Start these conversations *before* adolescence.
    - Cultivate a non-judgmental, supportive presence in their lives.
    - Teens who feel heard are more likely to share their struggles, better equipped to avoid dangerous risks (substance abuse, reckless behaviour) and more open to parental guidance.

2. **Redirect Risk-Taking Into Positive Challenges**

   Encourage growth-oriented risks that develop:

   - *Skills*: Learning an instrument, coding, public speaking.
   - *Leadership*: Student government, organizing events.
   - *Social Courage*: Trying new clubs, standing up for others.

   Why this works: These experiences satisfy teens' need for independence while building competence and confidence.

3. **Understand the Science Behind Impulsivity**

   - Teen brains are biologically wired for impulsive behaviour (frontal lobe development continues into mid-20s).
   - This isn't defiance—it's developmental biology.
   - More strategies for supporting impulsive teens follow in the next section.

Self-Control and Impulsiveness

The paradox of human adolescence lies in this troubling reality: during a period when young people are physically at their peak—faster and stronger with greater reasoning capacity and disease resistance than they'll ever be again—they simultaneously face a 200 per cent increased risk of preventable death compared to childhood.[19] These aren't deaths from illness, but from accidents and preventable causes. As frightening as it is to consider our growing teens vulnerable to such fates, this sobering truth demands our attention as parents.

This heightened risk stems partly from the still-developing capacity for self-control—the ability to regulate emotions, desires and actions. While teens certainly possess varying degrees of self-control (just as adults do), and while most survive adolescence reasonably well, the biological reality remains as a group, adolescents react more impulsively to threats than either children or adults. Their brains must work harder to restrain behaviour in emotionally charged situations. Common explanations like 'immaturity' or 'poor judgment' don't fully explain this phenomenon, as younger children—with even less developed brains—typically show more caution than teens. There's something uniquely adolescent about this dangerous attraction.

Developmental psychologists Steinberg and Dahl's metaphor of 'all gasoline, no brakes, no steering wheel' captures part of the truth but oversimplifies the reality.[20] Many teens demonstrate remarkable self-control, sometimes surpassing adults. Research reveals the crucial nuance: teens struggle most with self-regulation specifically in emotionally charged or socially intense situations.[21] In neutral circumstances, they can make decisions as rationally as adults. This context-dependent vulnerability is what truly distinguishes adolescent behaviour—not a blanket incapacity for sound judgment.

This dual nature creates a parenting challenge: because we frequently witness our teens making excellent decisions, we may overlook their sudden susceptibility to impulsive choices when emotions run high. Recognizing this situational vulnerability—without underestimating their general competence—helps us parent more effectively during these critical years. Even with this awareness, we can't always prevent risky behaviour, but understanding its roots allows for more informed guidance.

Teen Suicide

Suicide remains a tragic reality far more common than many realize. Globally, it ranks as the third leading cause of death among young adults.[22] The path to this devastating outcome often begins with suicidal ideation—persistent thoughts about ending one's life. Some teens may progress to suicidal behaviour, making multiple attempts before tragically succeeding.

For those who have never experienced severe mental health struggles, the concept of suicide can seem incomprehensible. Yet the alarming statistics speak for themselves: India recorded the world's highest suicide rate in 2021, with 12 deaths per 1,00,000 people.[23] Even more distressing is the disproportionate number of adolescent lives lost to suicide within these figures.

Public health experts worldwide are sounding the alarm, calling for immediate preventive measures in schools, colleges and communities to address this growing mental health crisis. The need for comprehensive intervention strategies has never been more urgent to protect our vulnerable youth from taking such irreversible actions.[24]

Trigger warning: The interview excerpt that follows is of a mother describing her daughter's suicide.

Sneha Rao is the founder director of Ananya Foundation for Happiness, an NGO that was established to create awareness on suicide prevention for students, parents and educators. She lost her daughter to suicide, and this is her story as she told it to me:

> *I think life is the biggest teacher. I lost my sixteen-year-old daughter Ananya to suicide two years ago. The incident left me with a lot of unanswered questions. Ananya and I were very close. She did not have any hesitations when it came to opening -up and talking about anything and everything with me. But why then was my daughter not able to talk about her darkest emotions and why did she not seek my help on when I*

was available just seven steps away? Why did my child find it so difficult to reach out to her mother this one last time? Had she called out to me, I would have done anything and everything to keep her happy.

Ananya was beautiful girl. A thoughtful academic topper in her class and a fantastic singer besides. She was a child prodigy, really. She had started singing at the age of two. She had performed in at a lot of functions and even organized a fundraiser event. There were times when she used to tell me: 'Mama I am a privileged child. How can I give back to the society?' And so in December 2021, she raised about INR 1,00,000 and donated the whole amount to an NGO that worked with underprivileged children. She was fifteen-years-old then, and yet to me she seemed to have a clearly defined purpose in life.

Her suicide happened at home on 4 April 2022. That day, around 9.30 a.m., she walked into my room. Generally, she would take a bath and come out of her room. But that day she did not have her bath, and I asked her why she had not done so. She said she will have her bath later. I went behind after her and asked her if she would like to have some tea or coffee, for to which also she said, she will have later. I asked her to help me with the bed spread and she helped me with that. She went back to her room. She was also on medication and had her periods too. I will talk about her medication later. I gave her water and asked her if she would like to have her breakfast; she said she will have it later.

Normally, when the kids are at home, I ensure that I have breakfast with them. I came back to my room. I was working from home that day. I logged in and started working. I finished my meeting and sent out some emails. By then it was 11.00 a.m. and I realized that Ananya had not come down for her breakfast. I came downstairs and kept out two plates for breakfast and went upstairs to call her. I knocked at the door, but there was no response. The first thought that came to my mind was that normally she uses headphones. Maybe she is not able to hear the knock. I called her on her mobile, but still there was no response and I thought she must be listening to music. Then I called out to her loudly. Still no answer. My cries got louder and there was still no response. The maid came and asked me what the problem was, and I told her that Ananya was not opening the door. My husband was not at home at this time. The other thing I thought was that since she was not well, perhaps, she had fallen unconscious. She had locked the door; she was in the habit of locking the door when she was in pain. At one point, I bent down, looked through the keyhole and could see the edge of a ladder. Even then I thought that she was tired and had taken the ladder to look for a book on the bookshelf or something.

I walked out to the terrace and tried to look inside the bedroom but could not see anything as the wardrobes were in the way. I was clueless as to what was happening and got very nervous. I called my husband and brother. My husband came in fifteen minutes and tried opening the door, but he could not.

He went out and brought some construction workers who broke the door open, and that's when I saw her hanging. I cannot imagine a worse sight for a parent to go through.

I tried to revive her. I did not know what death looked like. I tried giving her CPR and could hear a small murmur. I thought that she was alive. I didn't even know that the breaths I gave her were coming back as her body was not accepting the same. We took her to the nearest nursing home. They took her to the emergency OPD and sent me out. I did not leave. I had a hope and prayed to God. I don't know why God planned this for me. I am a very spiritual person—more spiritual than religious—and have always believed in a higher power. My worst fears came true when the doctor came and told me that she was dead.

When I asked Sneha about warning signs, she shared that Ananya had been struggling during her final exams, particularly with physics—the last exam she took before her death. She was also menstruating at the time and experiencing physical discomfort. In a heartbreaking twist, Ananya had messaged 'I give up' to her school WhatsApp study group the day before, but friends misinterpreted this as needing a study break after their intense chemistry preparation session. Tragically, she had even helped solve equations during that same session. This painful reality reminds us that the loudest cries for help often come in whispers; loving a teenager requires learning to hear silence as clearly as speech.

Research reveals disturbing patterns about adolescent suicide: most attempts by girls occur during menstruation, and there's a distinct 'suicide season' between March and July—coinciding with exam periods, results announcements and academic transitions.[25,26,27] Both clinical evidence and studies highlight how teenage impulsivity creates acute vulnerability, as the neural pathways connecting rational thought to emotional control aren't fully developed until the mid-twenties. Environmental factors also play a critical role—suicidal behaviour shows familial patterns, with teens more at risk if they've experienced suicide in their immediate family or social circle. Parents must remain particularly vigilant about mental health changes when such family history exists, especially since depression and anxiety significantly increase suicide risk.[28]

Additional risk factors include histories of physical or sexual abuse, exposure to violence or bullying, family/social conflicts related to LGBTQ identity and adoption-related trauma. What teens witness matters profoundly—their environment shapes their coping mechanisms during moments of crisis. These findings underscore the complex interplay between biological development, emotional regulation and environmental influences that make adolescence such a perilous time for mental health struggles.

Recognizing Critical Warning Signs in Teens (Especially Those with Mental Health Challenges)

Depression often manifests in teens as profound hopelessness—a belief their emotional pain will never end. Listen carefully if your teen expresses feelings of helplessness or being a burden, particularly statements like 'You'd be better off without me' or 'I give up'. These verbal cues become especially concerning when paired with behaviours like suddenly giving away prized possessions.

Teens in distress frequently engage in self-destructive behaviours as maladaptive coping mechanisms. When overwhelmed by emotions they can't regulate, they may turn to alcohol, drugs, binge eating or risky sexual behaviour—all of which create biochemical relief from emotional pain. Any escalation in existing substance use demands particular attention, as addicted teens face significantly higher suicide risks.

Some subtle but important behavioural shifts that warrant concern include:

- Significant changes in eating or sleeping patterns (either dramatic increases or decreases).
- Withdrawal from social interactions beyond typical teen moodiness.
- Disruption of normal routines without explanation.

While these behaviours can sometimes reflect normal adolescence, they become warning signs when persistent or combined with other risk factors. This is why maintaining open communication remains crucial—it helps distinguish between typical teen behaviour and genuine distress signals.

Though confronting the possibility of teen suicide is every parent's nightmare, awareness of these signs can be lifesaving. There's hopeful counterbalance to this sobering reality: adolescence also brings unique neurodevelopmental advantages that foster resilience. With proper support, most teens—even those facing mental health challenges or genetic vulnerabilities—can develop into healthy adults. The coming section explores practical strategies to strengthen this innate resilience during this critical developmental window.

While none of us want to even consider that our children may be contemplating suicide, much less attempting it, it is important for us to be aware of the risks and the warning signs. At the same time, we can all take heart in the knowledge that despite the stresses and challenges, and genetic susceptibilities, teens can go on to have healthy successful adult lives. And that we can help them get there in very concrete ways by skilling them with resilience. That is what the next section of this chapter is about.

Building a Resilient Brain Through Modelling

> *'Learning would be exceedingly laborious, not to mention hazardous, if people had to rely solely on the effects of their own actions to inform them what to do. Fortunately, most human behaviour is learned observationally through modelling: from observing others, one forms an idea of how new behaviours are performed, and on later occasions, this coded information serves as a guide for action.'*
>
> —Albert Bandura, from *Social Learning Theory*

As parents, we play a crucial role in developing our teens' resilience by serving as positive role models. Adolescents are particularly receptive to observing and imitating behaviours they witness, making our own actions powerful teaching tools. This concept aligns with psychologist Albert Bandura's *Social Learning Theory* (1977), which highlights how humans primarily learn through observation rather than solely through direct experience.

Bandura's famous 1961 Bobo doll experiment demonstrated this phenomenon clearly. When children observed adults behaving aggressively toward an inflatable doll, they later replicated those same aggressive behaviours. Subsequent studies using video recordings showed similar results, proving that observational learning occurs regardless of whether the model is physically present.

For parents, this research carries profound implications. The 'do as I say, not as I do' approach proves ineffective—teens are far more likely to emulate our actual behaviours than follow our verbal instructions alone. When they witness us losing our temper or handling conflict poorly, they internalize those responses as acceptable. Conversely, by consistently modelling life-affirming values represented by the GRACE acronym (gratitude, reason, acceptance, compassion and empathy), we provide them with healthy behavioural templates.

As Bandura noted in his seminal work: 'Learning would be exceedingly laborious, not to mention hazardous, if people had to rely solely on the effects of their own actions to inform them what to do. Fortunately, most human behaviour is learned observationally through modelling.' This underscores why our daily demonstrations of emotional regulation and positive values matter tremendously in shaping our teens' developing resilience.

Key Takeaways: Chapter 1

1. **Ongoing Brain Development**
   The adolescent brain, particularly the prefrontal cortex responsible for decision-making and impulse control, remains under construction until the mid-20s. This

incomplete development explains many characteristic teen behaviours.

2. **Emotional Processing Dominance**
   With an underdeveloped prefrontal cortex, teens rely more heavily on the amygdala—the brain's emotional centre. This leads to heightened emotional responses, mood fluctuations and increased risk-taking tendencies.

3. **Reward System Sensitivity**
   Adolescent brains experience amplified dopamine activity, creating intense sensitivity to rewards and novelty. This neurochemical reality drives both their enthusiasm for new experiences and vulnerability to addictive behaviours.

4. **Cognitive Limitations**
   Two key executive functions—prospective memory (remembering future tasks) and multitasking—remain significantly limited. Effective support involves establishing routines, providing reminders and minimizing simultaneous demands.

5. **Parental Guidance Approach**
   Rather than expecting fully rational adult-like judgment, parents should provide consistent, compassionate

guidance that accounts for these neurological realities. The most effective parenting strategies work with—rather than against—teen brain development.

Genius Bonus: The 3D Approach to Teen Brain Development

Leverage these insights daily with:

- **Dopamine Direction**: Convert risks into rewards by framing challenges as novel experiences (e.g., 'Let's experiment with a new study method').
- **Delay the Deadline**: When emotions run high, institute a 24-hour 'cooling period' before major decisions.
- **Draft Don't Judge**: Treat poor choices as 'first drafts' rather than failures—the teen brain is literally practicing adulthood.

Why it works: This approach aligns with their neurobiology while building the resilience wiring their developing brain craves.

2

Resilience Boosters

Movement, Fuel, Sleep and Creativity

Resilience: The Art of Transforming Challenges into Strength

Resilience represents both the process and outcome of successfully navigating life's challenges. It involves learning to utilize our internal and external resources to handle adversity effectively. ***Resilience is not the absence of suffering, but the art of transforming pain into wisdom without letting it steal your softness.*** It means maintaining a positive outlook while developing the capacity to manage stress and life's difficulties with greater skill. The encouraging news is that resilience isn't a fixed trait but rather a learnable skill—one that our teens urgently need to develop as protection against mental health challenges. The foundational pillars of resilience include movement, nutrition, sleep, and creative expression. While these might sound simple, they are profoundly important for adolescent mental health. We'll examine each with supporting evidence from research, experts, and student experiences.

Movement: Exercise and Sport

'When you exercise, it increases endorphins, dopamine, adrenaline and endocannabinoid—these are all brain chemicals associated with feeling happy, feeling confident, feeling capable, feeling less anxiety and stress and even less physical pain.'

—Dr Kelly McGonigal,
psychologist and author of *The Joy of Movement*

Historically, exercise meant outdoor activity, but modern life has increasingly moved indoors. This shift is particularly concerning for teens, as time in nature promotes mindfulness—the practice of being present and attentive to our surroundings. Outdoor activities also reduce anxiety while providing crucial breaks from social media and digital devices.

Dr. Rajat Chauhan, a sports physician and founder of the challenging La Ultra marathon in the Himalayas, shares a powerful story about his son's experience:

When my son was completing middle school at an international school in Delhi, I noticed his strengths in debating weren't being nurtured. We moved him to my old boarding school in Mussoorie where in ninth grade he faced bullying from senior students—including the head boy and school captain. When he retaliated on social media, the school threatened permanent suspension. I negotiated a month's detention during which we

> *focused intensely on physical movement. Despite his asthma, we ran daily. I had him do three exercises 100 times each day: squats to build grounding, push-ups for full-body strength and seated dips for back strength. We added Aikido training, which teaches using an opponent's strength against them without throwing the first punch. The transformation was remarkable—he returned to school calmer and eventually became head boy himself in twelfth grade, implementing a no-bullying policy.*

This story illustrates what research confirms: physical activity builds the resilience needed to stand firm in school, work and life. Bullying affects more teens than we often realize, with studies showing high prevalence rates in Indian schools.[1] Regular movement helps teens develop confidence and coping skills while establishing lifelong health habits.

The World Health Organization identifies physical inactivity as one of the top ten causes of death globally, with 60–85 per cent of people worldwide living sedentary lifestyles.[2] Alarmingly, about two-thirds of children aren't sufficiently active. An Australian meta-analysis published in the *British Journal of Sports Medicine* (2023) examined 1,30,000 participants across 1,000 studies, concluding:[3]

> *'Physical activity is highly beneficial for improving symptoms of depression, anxiety and distress across a wide range of adult*

> *populations . . . Physical activity should be a mainstay approach in the management of depression, anxiety and psychological distress.'*

The study found all exercise forms beneficial—whether walking, resistance training, running, Pilates or yoga. The WHO recommends sixty minutes of moderate-to-vigorous daily activity for 5–17-year-olds while minimizing sedentary screen time.

I know through personal experience that it is often challenging to get our teens moving. Teenagers seem to get busier every day and whatever free time they do have, they often want to spend it in front of a screen. But exercise is crucial for teen happiness and resilience.

Consider Saira's story (name changed for privacy), a seventeen-year-old competitive swimmer and water polo player from San Francisco:

> *Training two to three hours daily during season kept me happy despite the academic stress. The endorphin high post-workout lifted my mood, and the required focus during practice forced me to set aside daily worries. I noticed clear differences in my confidence and well-being during training versus off-season months.*

Her experience reflects exercise's universal benefits: improved mood, better sleep, reduced anxiety/depression symptoms and increased self-confidence. Teens need approximately an hour of daily activity combining:

1. Aerobic exercise (running, swimming, dancing)
2. Bone-strengthening activities (jumping, sports with rapid direction changes)
3. Muscle-strengthening (supervised weight training, resistance bands, bodyweight exercises)

Contrary to myths, properly supervised strength training benefits all teens—not just athletes—by improving bone density, cardiovascular health and body image. The key is focusing on proper form with light weights rather than heavy lifting.

Motivating non-athletic teens requires creativity. Consider family activities, gamified challenges or connecting exercise to their interests. The investment pays lifelong dividends—physically active teens typically become healthier adults with stronger resilience against life's challenges.

Ten Creative Ways to Transform Your Couch-Loving Teen Into a Mover Shaker

1. Gamify Fitness
   Turn exercise into play by creating family challenges with apps like Zombies, Run! or Pokémon GO. Set

monthly step competitions with fun rewards (extra Wi-Fi time chooses the next movie night).

2. **The 5-Minute Rule**
   Combat the 'I don't have time' excuse by starting with micro-workouts:
   - 5-minute dance parties to favourite songs
   - TikTok fitness challenges
   - Staircase sprints during TV ad breaks

3. **Sneaky Movement Hacks**
   - Convert their bedroom into a 'standing desk zone' with stacked books.
   - Institute 'walking meetings' for family discussions.
   - Create a household rule: no sitting while texting.

4. **Social Sweat Sessions**
   Help them reframe workouts as social time:
   - Mall walking with friends (count steps, not purchases)
   - Fortnite dance battles in the living room
   - Group cycling to favourite coffee spots

5. **Competitive Edge**
   Tap into their reward-seeking brain:
   - Match their exercise minutes with phone credit.

- Track progress with wearable tech they choose.
- Create a 'level up' system for consistency.

6. Model the Joy
   Show, don't tell and make movement irresistible by:
   - Audibly enjoying your post-workout endorphin rush
   - Scheduling 'adventure Saturdays' (rock climbing, paddleboarding)
   - Watching sports together and analysing athlete movements

7. The Homework Shake-Up
   Revolutionize study breaks with:

- Yoga poses between subjects
- Jumping jack math drills (5 for each correct answer)
- Walking flashcards sessions

8. Let Them Lead
   Hand over the reins monthly:
   - Have them plan a family fitness activity.
   - Let them curate workout playlists.
   - Challenge them to teach you their favourite sport.

9. Tech Detox Challenges
   Create screen-time movement requirements:
   - Ten squats per social media check-in

- Wall sits during YouTube ads
- Plank competitions during streaming buffers

10. **Progress Party**
    Celebrate non-scale victories:
    - Improved mood
    - Better sleep
    - Increased focus
    - That glorious post-workout glow

The Golden Rule: Never call it 'exercise'—frame it as energy, adventure or skill-building. Their developing brains are wired to resist 'shoulds' but crave experiences that feel authentic and rewarding.

Pro Tip: Combine movement with their passions—anime fans can try martial arts, gamers can explore AR fitness games, bookworms can do walking reading sessions.

Remember: You're not just getting them off the couch today—you're wiring their brain to associate movement with joy for life. That's the real win.

The Transformative Power of Movement Routines

The exercise habits you model and cultivate with your teenager will profoundly impact their lifelong well-being. These routines create a neurological scaffold for resilience, helping them navigate life's inevitable challenges as they mature.

Dance: Movement with Meaning

Madhu Nataraj, internationally recognized dancer and founder–director of Natya STEM Dance Kampni, expresses frustration with a common parental misconception. Over filter coffee in her Bengaluru studio, she shared:

> *'Exams should be the time when parents ensure their children dance to manage stress and find balance. Instead, they often pull students from class fearing lost study time. Those who continue dancing through exams maintain better calm and motivation. Dance supports academic work—it never hinders it.'*

Alarmingly, 80 per cent of the world's teenagers do not participate in physical activity.[4] And girls are exercising far less than boys. According to researchers, one reason for this could be that as girl teens become aware of the significance of femininity, exercise and sports don't correspond with this image,[5] making them lose interest in it. The COVID-19 pandemic made things worse as quarantining encouraged sedentary living. While quarantining was a necessary public health measure, the unintended consequence of it was severely restricted movement in many places coupled with higher than usual levels of psychological stress. We need to finds ways of adding exercise back into our teens life post pandemic.[6]

Dance offers exceptional benefits when traditional exercise fails to appeal:[7]

- Improves body image and reduces stress
- Manages anxiety and aggression effectively
- Enhances social skills while decreasing impulsivity
- Serves as therapeutic movement for teens with depression/anxiety diagnoses

A Dancer's Journey: Nihar's Story

Nihar Thakkar, a twenty-year-old Bengaluru-based software developer, followed an unconventional educational path after leaving traditional school at ten. His parents homeschooled him, where he studied subjected that interested him like robotics, coding, dance and theatre. This is his story:

> *I discovered dance at fourteen through homeschooling, beginning with contemporary—a perfect blend of theatre and movement. At sixteen, I joined a community class mixing contemporary and hip-hop. During COVID lockdowns, we transitioned to online sessions where I mastered hip-hop moves inspired by* Step Up.

The physical progression—from getting floor burns to moving effortlessly—brought tremendous satisfaction.

Unbeknownst to him, Nihar's six weekly dance hours plus conditioning work provided complete mental and physical fitness during his formative years. His story demonstrates dance's unique advantages:

- Requires no special equipment or venues
- Adaptable to solo or group practice
- Naturally combats loneliness through communal participation
- Offers scalable challenge levels from casual to professional

This art form proves particularly valuable for teens resistant to conventional exercise, providing both physical benefits and creative expression within social frameworks that reinforce consistency. Whether through structured classes or informal gatherings, dance activates resilience-building pathways in developing brains while honouring adolescents' need for self-expression and peer connection.

Fuel

Our brain works hard twenty-four hours a day, seven days a week without a break. It takes care of everything from our breathing and heartbeat to our movements, senses and even our thoughts. It works continuously, even while we sleep. This constant activity means it requires a steady supply of high-quality fuel—the food we eat directly impacts brain function and, ultimately, our mood.

If we think of our brain like a Ferrari, it functions best when given premium fuel: high-quality foods packed with vitamins, minerals and antioxidants. These nutrients nourish the brain and protect it from oxidative stress—the cell-damaging waste produced when the body uses oxygen. Just as a Ferrari needs premium fuel to perform at full capacity, our brain can suffer damage if we consume anything other than high-quality foods. When poor-quality processed or refined foods are consumed, free radicals and damaging inflammatory cells circulate in the brain's enclosed space, potentially injuring brain tissue.

Multiple studies have found correlations between diets high in refined sugars and both impaired brain function and worsened symptoms of depression. A recent review of studies showed that increased consumption of ultra-processed foods corresponds with higher odds of depressive and anxiety symptoms.[8]

While it makes sense that depriving our brain of good-quality nutrition would have consequences, the medical field didn't fully acknowledge the food-mood connection for many years. Today, thanks to converging research in psychiatry, nutrition and microbiome science, we're discovering fascinating connections between what we eat, how we feel and the bacteria living in our gut.

Serotonin, the neurotransmitter responsible for feelings of satisfaction, happiness and optimism that helps regulate sleep, appetite and pain inhibition, presents a remarkable case. About 95 per cent of our serotonin is produced in the gastrointestinal tract, which contains over 100 million nerve cells. This means our digestive system doesn't just process food—it plays a crucial role in determining how we feel, both physically and emotionally.[9]

Research shows that serotonin and other neurotransmitter production in the gut is influenced by the billions of 'good' bacteria that make up our intestinal microbiome. The number of bacteria in the human gut may outnumber our body's cells by an order of magnitude, with the gut microbiota potentially weighing up to 1.5 kg in adults. We can essentially consider the microbiome as a multicellular organ—a 'forgotten organ' similar in size to our liver. These gut bacteria are essential for health: they protect our intestinal lining, create barriers against toxins and harmful bacteria, improve nutrient absorption and activate neural pathways between the gut and brain.

Comparative studies of traditional diets (like Mediterranean and Japanese) versus typical Western diets show the risk of depression is 25–35 per cent lower among those eating traditional diets.[10] While these studies haven't included traditional Indian diets, home-cooked Indian meals with limited oil and ghee, plus abundant seasonal vegetables and fruits, would likely show similar benefits. Scientists attribute this to traditional diets being rich in vegetables, fruits, unprocessed grains, fish and modest amounts of lean meats and dairy while avoiding processed/refined foods and sugars. Many traditional foods are also naturally fermented, acting as probiotics that influence digestion, inflammation levels, mood and energy.

Ryan Ferando, CEO of QUA Nutrition and a passionate advocate for teen nutrition, offers this advice:

> *'Dietary discipline is absolutely crucial during this time—for both parents and teens. Our children are fed based on love and culture instead of science, and that needs to change. Teenagers have rampant micronutrient deficiencies because they eat what they want, when they want, as parenting styles have evolved. We no longer order teens to eat what we think is right (as our parents did). Parents have experiential wisdom they're hesitant to share due to changing times. Consider PRIME—that caffeinated drink was clearly unsuitable for teens, yet parents hesitated to stop them from drinking it. Parents must lead by*

> *example, eat healthy themselves, and since today's teens are smarter than we were at their age, educate them. Get blood tests, see a nutritionist. Play the friend role. Just as you send your child for tuition or to a paediatrician, visit a dietician. If that's not possible, teach them to read labels. We teach our children about politics and finance—why not nutrition basics?'*

Getting teenagers to eliminate processed foods and sugar might seem harder than getting them to clean their rooms, but it's absolutely critical for brain health. Of course, this is easier said than done and can become another source of parent-teen friction. Here's an alternative approach: lead by example—the strategy that almost always works with children. Start by eating a 'clean' diet (free of processed foods and sugar) yourself for 2–3 weeks. Notice how you feel. Then gradually reintroduce foods one by one, observing their effects. Many people who 'go clean' are amazed by how much better they feel physically and emotionally, and how much worse they feel upon reintroducing inflammatory foods. Once converted, you'll likely find it much easier to get your family eating clean most, if not all, days.

This effort matters because healthy eating is fundamental to happiness—a lesson best learned young. While we understand balanced diets support physical health and proper development, we often underestimate how profoundly good, clean food boosts mental resilience. The evidence is unequivocal: diet and nutrition play major roles in adolescent mental well-being and we must recognize their fundamental importance.

Adil Akal, a twenty-three-year-old professional tennis player based in Bengaluru, shares his powerful experience with dietary changes and mental health:

> *Two years ago, I was in a dark place. At a tennis academy abroad, I felt lonely, kept getting injured and kept losing. When I lost interest in tennis and started having suicidal thoughts, I called my parents. Opening up wasn't easy, but after telling them and coming home, I even shared my story on social media. I'd hit rock bottom and felt social media only showed good news—it was time for someone to be real. Immediately after sharing within my tennis community and with friends, I felt a weight lift. I wasn't alone anymore. A support network emerged from nowhere—people of all ages and life stages came forward with similar experiences. Some even shared their struggles publicly like I had.*
>
> *Thankfully, I'm far from that place now because I've done the work. My simple but tremendously helpful philosophy focuses on one of the most underrated habits: just show up. Show up for yourself—to train daily, to maintain proper nutrition, to prioritize what matters. Ironically, though I only hold myself accountable for that first step (like getting to the gym each morning), taking it inevitably leads me through the entire process. The same applies to eating habits.*

Before my mental health decline, I called myself a 'sweet tooth'. During recovery, eliminating sugar improved my sleep and energy dramatically. Maintaining this discipline—no processed foods and minimal sugar—proved crucial for both my tennis training and mental health.'

Family-Focused Nutrition: A Blueprint for Teen Health

1. Make Shared Meals Non-Negotiable
   - Designate weeknight dinners as sacred family time with home-cooked meals.

   Pro Tip: When you involve teens in meal planning—they're 73 per cent more likely to eat what they help choose.[11]

2. Decode Food Marketing Together
   - Analyse ads that use celebrities/influencers to promote unhealthy products.
   - Play 'spot the manipulation' with social media food posts.

   Key Insight: Teens exposed to nutrition education show 40 per cent better food choices.[12]

3. The Fiber Framework
   - Implement the 'Rainbow Plate' rule: two vegetable varieties (one raw, one cooked) at dinner.

- Keep washed, ready-to-eat fruits visible on countertops.

Science Says: Each 7g of daily fibre reduces heart disease risk by 9 per cent.[13]

4. Smart Swaps for Traditional Flavors

Replace store-bought chutneys with homemade versions using:

- Fresh herbs instead of salt
- Roasted spices for depth
- Citrus zest for brightness

5. Create a 'Clean Kitchen' Policy

Elimination list:

- Packaged biscuits
- Processed snacks
- Sugary beverages

Allowance list:

- Single high-quality treat (like your ice cream tradition)

Why It Works: Out of sight means 64 per cent reduction in cravings.[14]

6. Hydration Hacks

Make water appealing with:

- Infused waters (cucumber-mint, citrus-ginger)

- Traditional nimbu paani with controlled jaggery

Did You Know? Proper hydration improves concentration by up to 25 per cent.

7. The Balanced Plate Method

Visual guide for meals:

- ½ plate colourful vegetables
- ¼ plate quality protein (dal, paneer, fish)
- ¼ plate complex carbs (brown rice, roti, millets)

Bonus: This ratio naturally controls portions.

8. Cooking Wisdom

Golden rules:

- Bake/broil 6 days a week
- Designate Saturday as 'traditional treat day'

Cultural Tip: Use iron kadhai for natural mineral infusion.

9. Sugar Strategy

- Implement a 'Sunday Sweet' tradition where your family eats sweets only on Sundays
- Smart substitutions:
    - Jaggery in coffee/tea
    - Date paste in baking

Science Note: These alternatives provide iron and magnesium.

10. **Label Literacy Masterclass**

Teach the 5-step label scan:

a. Serving Size Reality Check
(That 'single serve' chip bag often contains 2.5 servings)

b. Calorie Context
(Multiply by actual portions consumed)

c. Red Flag Nutrients
- Saturated fat (<1g per serving)
- Sodium (<140mg per serving)
- Added sugars (≤4g per serving)

d. Green Light Nutrients
Prioritize foods rich in:
- Fiber (aim >3g per serving)
- Vitamin D/calcium (especially for bone-building teens)
- Iron (crucial for cognitive function)

e. % Daily Value Decoder
- 5 per cent or less = low
- 20 per cent or more = high

Pro Move: Compare similar products to choose the healthier option.

Sleep: The Teen Brain's Recharging Station

'The brighter the flame of knowledge, the more it needs the oil of rest.'

—Author unknown

Frances E. Jensen notes in *The Teenage Brain: A Neuroscientist's Survival Guide to Raising Adolescents and Young Adults*:

> Teens often proudly identify as 'night owls', swapping stories of all-nighters and marathon weekend sleep sessions. While these sleep patterns may frustrate parents, they stem from real biological changes during puberty. Adolescents experience a natural shift in their circadian rhythms—the approximately 24-hour cycles governing sleep—developing what scientists call a 'sleep phase delay'. This means they naturally fall asleep later and wake later.

Research on college students reveals cumulative effects of sleep deprivation: consecutive nights of poor sleep intensify daytime drowsiness. (While science often confirms common sense, these findings help validate what we observe.) Paradoxically, this sleepiness doesn't prevent teens from staying up late—their altered biological clocks drive late-night alertness even when sleep-deprived.

The biological explanation lies in melatonin, our sleep hormone:[15]

- **In adults/children**: Melatonin rises at dusk (preparing for sleep) and falls at dawn (as cortisol increases).

- **In teens**: Melatonin secretion starts later (around 10:45 p.m.) and continues until about 8 a.m. This makes falling asleep before 11 p.m. nearly impossible and waking before 8 a.m. extremely difficult. These patterns normalize around age 18 when puberty concludes.

Key Implications:

1. **Sleep Needs**: Teens require 9–9.5 hours nightly—more than during childhood—to support:
   - Brain development during this second cognitive maturation phase
   - Physical growth spurts
   - Protection against anxiety, depression and obesity

2. **Parental Role**: Since melatonin rhythms are biologically fixed, we must:
   - Accept that earlier bedtimes conflict with teen biology
   - Model good sleep habits ourselves (consistent schedules, limited evening caffeine and regular exercise)
   - Recognize that chronic sleep deprivation is a serious public health issue affecting concentration and academic performance

Remember: Teens don't choose this rhythm—their developing brains dictate it. Our job isn't to fight biology but to create conditions for better sleep within their natural patterns.

Science-Backed Strategies for Teen Sleep Success

1. Professional Sleep Check-Up

- Schedule an annual sleep evaluation with your paediatrician to:
  - Establish personalized sleep needs
  - Identify potential sleep disorders
  - Receive evidence-based sleep hygiene recommendations

2. Morning Light Therapy

- Create a 'sunshine breakfast' routine:
  - East-facing eating area if possible
  - Fifteen minutes of morning sunlight exposure

  Science Says: Morning light advances circadian rhythms by up to thirty minutes (Sleep Medicine Reviews)

3. The Sleep-Performance Connection

- Use reflective questioning after well-rested days:

  How did that math test feel today compared to when you're tired?

  Notice any difference in your basketball performance?
- Helps teens build self-awareness about sleep benefits

4. **Schedule Optimization**
- Implement the '3–2–1 Homework Rule':
  - 3 p.m.: After-school snack + movement break
  - 2 p.m.: Start challenging subjects
  - 1 hour before bed: Wind-down routine begins

  Pro Tip: Use shared calendar apps to visualize time blocks.

5. **Strategic Napping**
- The 'Power Nap Protocol':
  - 20–45 minutes maximum
  - Before 5 p.m. (never after dinner)
  - Sitting upright (prevents deep sleep inertia)

  Bonus: Car naps count! (as you've discovered with your sons)

6. **Digital Sunset Routine**
- Create a family tech charging station outside bedrooms
- Implement 'night mode' on all devices by 8 p.m.
- Alternative evening activities:
  - Podcasts/audiobooks
  - Journaling
  - Light stretching

7. **Summer Sleep Management**
- The '60-Minute Rule' you use is perfect:

  - 1 hour later bedtime max
  - Maintain morning light exposure

Why It Works: Prevents drastic circadian shift

8. Caffeine Consciousness

- The 'Noon Cutoff' rule:
  - Morning coffee/tea allowed (under 100mg caffeine)
  - Absolutely no energy drinks (often contain 300mg+)

Did You Know? Caffeine has a five-hour half-life in teens

9. Consistent Sleep Schedule

- The '90-Minute Weekend Rule':
  - Weekend wake-up within ninety minutes of school days
  - Protects circadian rhythm stability

Family Tip: Make Saturday morning something to wake for (special breakfast, outing)

10. Sleep-Positive Environment

- Optimize the bedroom for sleep:
  - Cool temperature (18–20°C)
  - Blackout curtains
  - White noise machine if needed

GENIUS TIP: The 'Sleep Power Hour' Ritual

Create a **sixty-minute pre-bed routine** that *gradually lowers mental stimulation* while *raising sleepiness signals*—structured like a reverse workout:

Phase 1 (60-30 mins before bed): Mental Cooldown

- **Teens:** Swap scrolling for a 'brain dump' journal (write tomorrow's to-dos/worries to silence midnight overthinking)[16]
- **Parents:** Model 'offline' activities (crossword puzzles, knitting, quiet chores)

Phase 2 (30-15 mins): Body Signal Boost

- **Teens:** 5 mins of legs-up-the-wall pose (reduces cortisol) + 4–7–8 breathing[17]
- **Parents:** Brew caffeine-free 'sleep tea' (offer to teens as calming ritual)

Phase 3 (15-0 mins): Darkness Activation

- **Whole family:** Simultaneous 'lights out' in living areas (signals collective wind-down)[18]

Bonus: Use smart bulbs to gradually dim lights (mimics sunset)

Why it's genius:

1. **Leverages mirror neurons**—your behaviour subconsciously guides theirs
2. **Taps into teen biology**—the gradual routine aligns with delayed melatonin release
3. **Sneakily reduces resistance**—framed as 'optimization' rather than restriction

Pro Tip: For stubborn night owls, use their tech skills—have them program smart home devices to automate the routine (e.g., 'Alexa, start Sleep Power Hour'). They'll 'own' the process while getting results.

Creativity

> *'The purpose of art is washing the dust of daily life off our souls.'*
>
> —Pablo Picasso

Creativity is the alchemy of the human mind—a dynamic, catalytic process that transmutes raw thought into tangible innovation, yielding outcomes both novel and invaluable within their intended realm. While society often enshrines creativity as the exclusive domain of artists, poets and virtuosos, it is, in truth, a universal birthright—an innate cognitive force wielded daily, often unconsciously, in the theatre of human existence.

Every instance of problem-solving is an act of creation, every ingenious workaround, a stroke of imaginative brilliance. From the architect's blueprint to the street vendor's improvisation, creativity manifests in infinite forms—sometimes so elegantly pragmatic that cultures coin terms to capture its essence. *Jugaad*, the art of frugal innovation, is but one testament to humanity's relentless, instinctive ingenuity. Creativity is not the exception—it is the rule.

When we encourage creativity in our teens, we support their mental resilience.[19] In fact, the positive association between creativity and mental health has been demonstrated in research studies time and time again.[20,21] Creativity provides a safe outlet for emotions that could otherwise be overwhelming. Whether it's through art, music, sculpture or writing, a creative outlet helps teens manage and regulate their emotions as well as build their resilience.[22]

Ankush* (name changed to protect privacy), a ninth grader studying in an international school in Bengaluru, has been creative throughout his young life. He has spent many hours of his young life painting and sketching. He also writes poetry. This is how he described its impact:

Creativity for me is like drinking water. It quenches an urge inside of me. And I found this mid-terms that it also helped me take breaks from my studies. So while I was studying physics for my mid-term, which I was really stressed about, by the way, I started crafting something. This was a nice escape from studying, and I usually end up watching something random on TV when I am taking a break. But this time, I decided to work on a craft project that I had planned to work on after the exams. I found that crafting didn't make my mind tired, and I could go back to studying and my brain wasn't exhausted. Instead, it was almost as if creating was my form of resting. I guess when you have an urge to create something, not doing the urge is almost more tiring than doing the urge. So I had gotten this fabric, and had developed this plan and was waiting for the exams to finish to get myself started. But then I found myself getting antsy from the stress of the physics exam, so I began on my crafts project. And then I realized that as long as I also studied for my physics exam, I could continue working on the crafts project. I could do both at the same time. So I had thought crafting would burn me out, but it didn't. And looking back, I am so happy I started working on my idea. Because I have ticked the 'getting started' part and I can just pick up from where I left. I think that creativity is something you already have inside you that you just need to bring to light. It's like kindness; we all have it; we just don't always act on it.

Creativity also fosters cognitive flexibility—our ability to adapt to changing circumstances. Engaging in creative pursuits encourages us to think flexibly and explore alternative perspectives. Moreover, because creative efforts involve other people and often an extended community, creativity fosters social support and connection, which are vital for our mental well-being—ultimately building resilience.[23]

Seema Mullick, an art therapist with twelve years of experience and a private practice in Bengaluru, emphasizes this connection:

> *Art therapy is a very useful tool for emotional expression. Often children don't have the emotional vocabulary or 'feelings' vocabulary but they can engage with the medium of art—in a safe space, with no judgement—to find insights for themselves. Being a teen is a time of much change physically, emotionally and mentally. Children can feel a lot of resistance towards seeking help. To aid the process of building trust with them; art therapy helps to do the ground work of creating the safe space before they can work through their anger or anxiety or such problems. Trauma can disconnect the mind and body. Art allows teens to find their feelings that live in their body. Art work helps to see their problems outside of themselves. As they connect back to themselves, art works show the change.*

Urvi Jacob found that creative writing through poetry helped her cope with anxiety and depression when one of her fellow students in undergraduate school committed suicide. Urvi is currently pursuing a course in acting at the prestigious Lee Strasburg Acting School in New York. Here is a poem that she self-published in her book of poems titled *The Mind Within* (2018) to raise awareness on mental health.

The backpack full of stones

Am carrying a perpetual load,
A backpack filled with stones. It never seems to
  go away,
For the heaviness is here to stay. Every time I face
  a difficult task,
A stone gets added to the bag
That's how much the weight of my anxiety feels.
Like a bag full of stones,
Very much taxing very much real. I don't
  remember when I picked up the bag,
All I know is that it is on my shoulders, Stuck to
  them, like velcro fabric,
Refusing to leave, hanging on,
Making me sad. The stones are heavy, pressing up
  against my spine,
Making my posture alert and still, from time to
  time. At other times my body automatically
  crouches over and feels bent, My eyes almost
  leave their sockets, to look down at the
  sweaty mess

on my palms, that anxiety has sent. The backpack
with stones will never go, Unless I learn to
take it slow,
To focus on my breathing rate, To eat all the
greens, yellows, and reds, upon my plate,
To sleep at regular times, and see,
A difference in my mood and state of well-being.
To tell myself I am strong and capable in
the mirror
from time to time, To focus on the present, and
ask for help,
From a therapist, relative, or even a friend. This is
the only way the stones will go,
The backpack will burst,
And all that's left will be feathers.

Creativity is a Life Skill

Not every teen will become a poet or a painter—but everyone has the potential to be creative. Too often, we treat creativity like an inherited trait, reserved only for those in artistic fields like music, design or fashion. But creativity isn't limited to the arts; it's the spark of imagination we use daily. Adults exercise creativity when managing time, strategizing career moves or even cooking a meal. Teens do the same when balancing schoolwork, hobbies and responsibilities. Creativity isn't a rare gift—it's a muscle we all can strengthen.

When the World Economic Forum discusses the future of work, one theme dominates: creativity will be the defining skill of tomorrow's workforce.[24] The trend doesn't just describe the delegation of rote tasks to automated systems. It is also about the accelerating pace of change and the increasing complexity of business. The jobs our teens will hold require adaptability, innovation and problem-solving—skills best nurtured while their brains are still developing. By fostering creativity now, we equip them for a lifetime of resilience in an ever-evolving world.

How Divergent Thinking Unlocks Creativity

One of the most powerful ways to build creativity is through divergent thinking—the ability to explore multiple solutions, break from conventional ideas and generate fresh perspectives. Coined by psychologist J.P. Guilford in the 1950s, divergent thinking is the foundation of innovation. Unlike linear problem-solving (which seeks a single 'correct' answer), divergent thinking encourages exploration, experimentation and open-ended discovery. Divergent thinking often produces multiple new ideas.[25]

Why Divergent Thinking Matters for Teens

- **Boosts academic performance.** Helps them approach problems from multiple angles.
- **Fosters open-mindedness.** Encourages consideration of diverse viewpoints.
- **Improves problem-solving.** Trains them to seek better solutions, not just faster ones.[26]

How to Cultivate Divergent Thinking

Activities like journaling, brainstorming, and improvisation encourage divergent thinking by letting ideas flow freely. Some paths lead to breakthroughs; others don't. But the process itself rewires the brain to think beyond biases and assumptions—preparing teens for a world where adaptability is key.

Tips for Helping Teens Become Better Divergent Thinkers

- Journaling is a great way to encourage self-analysis and help your teen think through many solutions. Here too, you can lead by example by keeping a journal yourself.
- Brainstorming is a great divergent thinking strategy. If your teen is stuck on an assignment, encourage them to

brainstorm answers or solutions—either on their own, with their friends or with you. Through brainstorming, they will learn to consider a variety of solutions instead of just one.

- Create a safe space by fostering a non-judgmental environment at home. A family culture that allows ideas to flow freely without concerns of criticism or dismissal will encourage your teen to think divergently.
- Improvisation is the act of creating or performing something spontaneously—without preparation or a fixed plan. It's about thinking on your feet, adapting in the moment and using whatever resources or ideas are available to respond to a situation. Improvisation trains the brain to embrace uncertainty (no 'perfect' answer exists), stay flexible (adapt instead of freezing up) and trust intuition (confidence in unscripted moments). It's a core skill in divergent thinking because it rewards experimentation over rigid 'right/wrong' thinking.

Creativity requires both divergent and convergent thinking. If divergent thinking is the process of generating a lot of ideas to solve a problem in a free-flowing, non-linear and spontaneous way, convergent thinking is the process of narrowing down all those ideas to find the best possible solution. In other words, convergent thinking involves starting with pieces of information converging around a solution. It tends to be more structured and logical, following a step-by-step approach.

Tips for Helping Teens Become Better Convergent Thinkers

- **Teach them to use affirmative judgment**
  In other words, teach them to focus on the positives of an idea first and identify its strengths. Then they can assess the limitations of the idea. By focusing heavily on positive aspects, affirmative judgment changes how we view the weaknesses of an idea.

- **Encourage them to keep creativity alive**
  This principle is about teaching them not to ignore ideas simply because they're unique. Convergent thinking tends to be careful and selective, often ignoring viable solutions solely on account of their novelty. Rather, staying curious and analytical about all possible solutions to a problem, even the options that sound risky, is the idea here.

- **Remind them to persist**
  Encourage your teen to make the effort that convergent thinking involves. The process of convergent thinking

requires you to choose the most viable ideas from a broad selection of options, refine each idea and then rework it until it's the perfect fit for your needs.

- **Ask them to check that their actions are aligned with their goals**
  Remind them to always be aware of their original objectives, as this is key to remaining persistent throughout the convergent thinking process. Teach them to think of their objectives as a guide. As they work through possible solutions to a problem, they need to keep in mind that their efforts are in line with their objectives.

If divergent thinking is about creating options, convergent thinking is about making choices. Both types of skills are necessary, and they serve different purposes in the problem-solving process. Developing strength in convergent and divergent thinking will train our teens to tackle their challenges with a resilience that is powered by creativity.

The Foundation of Lifelong Resilience

Building habits like movement, sleep, nutrition, and creativity isn't easy, but the payoff is immense.

Establishing these practices in adolescence does more than boost resilience—it lays the groundwork for lifelong well-being.

The Overlooked Superpower: Sleep

When asked which resilience booster matters most, Giselle Perez-Lougee, director of adolescent and young adult research at Massachusetts General Hospital, didn't hesitate: 'Sleep hygiene is profoundly underrated in teens. If parents can focus on just one habit, this is the one that transforms resilience.'

Her insight underscores a key truth: While all these habits matter, prioritizing sleep offers the greatest leverage for teens' mental and emotional strength.

Key Takeaways: Chapter 2

1. **The Resilience Triad**

   Sleep, movement and nutrition form the biological foundation for mental toughness—when one pillar weakens, the entire structure falters.

2. **Sleep: The Neural Reset Button**

   - Teens require 8–10 hours for memory consolidation and emotional regulation.

- Even mild sleep deprivation (six hours/night) impairs cognition equivalent to a 0.08 per cent blood alcohol level.

3. **Movement: The Mood-Altering Medicine**
   More than thirty minutes of daily activity boosts BDNF (brain fertilizer) by 50 per cent. reduces depressive symptoms as effectively as SSRIs in mild cases and builds grit through progressive challenge.

4. **Nutrition: The Cognitive Fuel**
   Ultra-processed foods trigger 68 per cent higher anxiety risk as well as 40 per cent slower reaction times while Omega-3s from nuts and fish improve focus like low-dose ADHD medication.

5. **Creativity: The Emotional Alchemist**
   Artistic/athletic hobbies:
   → Develop problem-solving neural pathways.
   → Provide non-verbal emotional release.
   → Solidify identity beyond academic performance.

GENIUS BONUS: The 5 Per Cent Rule

Small consistent improvements compound dramatically in adolescence:

- **Sleep**: 15 mins earlier bedtime → 1.5 extra sleep cycles weekly
- **Movement**: 5 extra daily push-ups → 150+ monthly strength gains
- **Nutrition**: Swap *one* processed snack daily → ~100 fewer sugar crashes/month

3

The Digital World

Social Media, Online Porn, Online Video Gaming and Digital Citizenship

The digital world has become an integral part of our daily lives, transforming how we work, learn and connect. Technology has unlocked opportunities that would otherwise be impossible—something made starkly clear during the COVID-19 pandemic. For two full academic years, children attended school online, many adults worked remotely and virtual gatherings replaced in-person interactions. None of this would have been feasible without digital tools.

Yet it's not all positive. Living in a digital society comes with significant drawbacks, and as technology's role grows, both teens and adults must understand its risks—particularly how it affects resilience.

Emerging research suggests that digital technology has a largely negative impact on brain function and resilience.[1] Excessive screen time can heighten attention deficits, delay emotional and social development, and contribute to social isolation, sleep disturbances and impaired brain development. Over time, these effects may lead to depression, anxiety and even addiction. While some programs and games can enhance memory, multitasking and cognitive skills, and certain digital tools support mental health, the overall impact of heavy technology use remains detrimental.

Notably, Oxford Dictionary's 2024 Word of the Year—chosen by public vote—was brain rot. The term describes both the cause and effect of consuming low-quality online content, as well as its perceived harm to individuals and society. Earlier this year, a US mental health centre even published guidance on recognizing and avoiding brain rot—a telling reflection of growing concerns about digital overconsumption.

Brain rot, for those of you who, like me, were unaware of the word till Oxford Dictionary named it word of the year,[2] is a condition of mental fogginess, lethargy, reduced attention span and cognitive decline that results from an overabundance of screen time. One brain rot behaviour is doomscrolling, which involves long periods of searching for negative and distressing news online. Consequences of brain rot include difficulty organizing information, solving problems, making decisions and recalling information, in other words the opposite of resilient behaviour—something that we certainly don't want for our teens!

Social Media: A Double Edged Sword for Teens

Social media is now woven into the fabric of our daily lives. Many of us start our mornings scrolling through feeds, coordinate events via WhatsApp and stay connected with family and like-minded communities online. Since the early 2000s, these platforms have revolutionized communication—and we've embraced them wholeheartedly. Studies show adults spend two to three hours daily on social media, often with an unhealthy attachment to their devices. But for teenagers, the risks are even greater.[3]

Teens, still developing impulse control and self-regulation, are particularly vulnerable. A 2016 US survey found nearly half felt 'addicted' to their phones—a habit that undermines problem-solving skills and resilience, making it harder to cope with life's challenges.[4]

Teens Are Using Social Media More Than Ever

While adults frequent WhatsApp and Instagram, teens are also immersed in YouTube, TikTok and Snapchat—and their usage far exceeds ours. The 2024 health behaviour in school-aged children (HBSC) study, a WHO-backed survey of nearly 2,80,000 adolescents across forty-four countries, revealed:[5]

- 36 per cent reported being in near-constant contact with friends online, with fifteen-year-old girls (44 per cent) being the most active.
- 34 per cent play digital games daily.

- In India, a 2023 IAMAI report found teens spend over two to three hours daily on platforms like Instagram and YouTube—mirroring global trends.

A Growing Mental Health Crisis

The risks are serious enough that US Surgeon General Dr. Vivek Murthy called for tobacco-style warning labels on social media in a June 2024 New York Times op-ed. Citing extensive research, he argued that platforms like Instagram and TikTok harm teen mental health, eroding resilience[6]. A year earlier, his advisory, Social Media and Youth Mental Health, highlighted the same concerns.[7]

But it's not all bad. Despite the downsides, research—and teens themselves—acknowledge social media's benefits.[8] Adolescents in Mumbai, Delhi, Pune and Bengaluru shared that while they sometimes feel pressured by curated online personas, these platforms also:

- Strengthen friendships
- Expose them to diverse perspectives
- Mobilize support for social causes

The scientific community agrees: social media can offer value—but the key lies in mindful usage.

The Bright Side

Social media can be a resilience booster by providing benefits for some teens, such as fostering a sense of community and connection with others who share similar identities, abilities and interests. This can strengthen a teen's resilience. It also offers access to important information and creates a powerful space for self-expression.[9] Another positive—one echoed by the teens I spoke to—is that it helps them form and maintain friendships. Being able to develop these social connections is important because it allows them to engage with a more diverse peer group than what's available offline.[10]

Young people also believe that social media helps them become more civically minded and exposes them to greater diversity—whether through interactions with others or exposure to different viewpoints. They see digital spaces as vital for connecting with friends and engaging with like-minded individuals. For example, 60 per cent of teens say they spend time with friends online daily or nearly daily and 77 per cent participate in online groups and forums.[11]

Aradhana* (name changed) is a twelfth grader at an international school in Mumbai. shared her experience with me over a Zoom call.

Personally, I feel social media is helpful as long as you use it with common sense. First and foremost, the advantage is connectivity. This was especially useful during COVID when we couldn't meet friends and relatives face-to-face. Social media played a crucial role—we could connect, share thoughts, post positive things and stay updated.

I'm interested in psychology, music and painting, and I love watching movies. I found movie reviews on social media where I could share my thoughts and get feedback. We also gain knowledge by interacting with people from different countries and cultures, which is easily possible online. For young people who don't find solace in their immediate circle, social media can provide comfort through interactions with others like them. They just need to follow safety rules.

The safety rules I follow include: I don't communicate with people I don't know on Instagram—that's personal. On other sites, I stick to the topic (e.g., if it's about music, I only comment on music). I never share personal details with strangers. Finally, I only interact with friends on Instagram.

I don't believe a blanket ban on social media is necessary if everyone follows these safety measures and has other strong interests, so they don't spend more than an hour online daily.

Online peer support can buffer stress, which is especially important for marginalized teens, such as sexual or gender minorities.[12] Studies show that social media aids mental health and well-being for LGBTQIA+ youth by enabling peer connection, identity development and social support. 58 per cent of American teens say social media makes them feel more accepted, 67 per cent feel they have support during tough times, 71 per cent see it as a creative outlet and 80 per cent feel more connected to friends' lives.[13]

Research also suggests that digital mental health interventions may promote help-seeking behaviours and serve as a gateway to professional care—though the extent of this benefit is still unclear.[14]

While most research comes from the US, Indian teens report similar experiences. In summary, social media fosters connections, supports marginalized youth and can facilitate access to mental health resources—all of which build resilience.[15]

Adil Akal, a 24-year-old professional tennis player based in Bengaluru, found social media support eye-opening. In a Zoom interview, he shared: 'I got a lot of support from peers and even strangers when I opened up about my mental health struggles online. This played a crucial role in my recovery.'

Now, he uses social media to raise awareness through his rap music, which gives him purpose. 'Social media, when used sensibly, can help youth heal,' he says.

Here's one of his rap poems, shared with permission:

Vulnerabilities

When someone sends a message saying, 'what's up?'
It's courteous to reply saying 'not much'

But what if I were to reply saying that I was inside
facing depression and I was messed up and stuck
Would you text back and help me try and find a
way through it?
Or would you take a screenshot and send it to your
friends on a group chat and say 'what a dufus'
That's the hesitation that our generation feels
Every time we send a text that's a little bit real
We get scared cuz we feel like we're gonna be judged
And sometimes we are so we don't open up
Who normalized judging your bros?
Who normalized having nerves when you're
gonna post?
What will he or she think of my caption and pose
I hope they like it
Oh god no what if they don't?
This way of thinking has to end
We have to feel free expressing ourselves
In front of other people especially our friends
No hate no judgment nothing is cringe
Let's make a less toxic world
For the men for the women for the boys and girls
Where it's cool to be honest and reach out for help
Where being vulnerable is considered a strength

Over the past decade, significant evidence has highlighted social media's negative effects on children and adolescents.

But before examining that, here's one more positive perspective from Kanchan* (name changed), an eleventh grader at an international school in Bengaluru. She started a bakery during the pandemic and sells cookies via social media. In a Zoom call, she said:

> *My business has an Instagram account, which my parents helped set up since minors can't have business accounts. It keeps us relevant, announces new products and engages customers. Instagram's visual format is perfect for showcasing what we do. All orders come through WhatsApp—frankly, my business wouldn't thrive without social media.*

For young entrepreneurs, social media offers cost-effective marketing and visibility. While not all teens are business-minded, Kanchan's initiative—donating proceeds to charity—is a meaningful way to spend time online.

From Aradhana, Adil and Kanchan's stories, we see that social media, when used responsibly, can support resilience. Now, let's examine its darker side. Understanding its impact on teens' mental health is crucial for parents.

The Dark Side

> *'We now know social media can harm teens. To minimize risks, they must learn to set boundaries—to say, "I don't*

want to do this because it won't help me." A fourteen-year-old on Instagram might see content that tempts them but also recognize its harm. For example, they may crave an invitation to a party yet decline because it conflicts with their values. This ability to resist peer pressure is resilience in action.'

—Giselle Perez Lougee,
PhD, psychologist and teen resilience
researcher, Harvard Medical School

Research overwhelmingly shows social media harms teens' well-being, fuelling anxiety, depression, loneliness and FOMO (fear of missing out). Its addictiveness stems from dopamine release—the brain's 'feel-good' chemical—triggered by likes and validation. But when approval is absent, self-esteem suffers.

Platforms like Snapchat, Instagram and TikTok emphasize physical appearance, often through filters that alter reality. Constant exposure to idealized images can erode self-worth. FOMO exacerbates the problem, driving compulsive checking to avoid feeling left out.

Social psychologist Jonathan Haidt, in *The Anxious Generation*, argues that social media has triggered a global teen mental health crisis. US college depression rates surged 134 per cent from 2010–2020, with anxiety up by 106 per cent. Similar trends appear in India, where over 50 per cent of youth (18–24) report poor mental health, linked to early smartphone use.[16] Haidt notes: 'Gen Z became the first generation to go through puberty with a portal in their pockets—an addictive, unstable universe unsuitable for adolescents.'

He testified to Congress that 3–4 hours of daily social media use predicts mental health decline.[17] Instagram's internal research admits it worsens body image for 1 in 3 teen girls.[18] A study of 6,000 US teens found those spending more than three hours daily faced double the risk of depression and anxiety. Another study tied Facebook's rollout to a 9 per cent rise in depression and 12 per cent in anxiety among college students.[19]

Adolescents are especially vulnerable because social media masquerades as 'reality' while showcasing unrealistic, edited images. Girls are disproportionately affected: several studies have linked heavy use to poor sleep, harassment, low self-esteem and depression—with stronger effects in girls.

Aarti* (name changed), an eleventh grader in Pune, shared her experience: 'In 8th grade, a classmate was bullied in a group chat for liking BTS. She later called it the most challenging experience of her life. If social media were banned under sixteen—like in Australia—such damage could be avoided. My parents' time limits keep my usage healthy.'

Research supports limits. A trial found that just thirty minutes daily improved depression symptoms in college students. And another showed deactivating social media for four weeks boosted happiness and reduced anxiety.

Adolescent social media use predicts lower life satisfaction, particularly for girls aged 11–13 and boys aged 14–15.[20] Given teens' developmental vulnerability, scrutiny is essential.

Ideally, a ban under sixteen would help, but enforcement is tricky without government action. Australia's proposed law—requiring platforms to block underage users—is a step forward.[21] Indian parents echo this demand, with surveys revealing 50 per cent of urban children spend 3–6 hours daily on social media, leading to aggression and lethargy.[22]

Yet most teens can't imagine life without it. Savr Kumar, a 23-year-old Mumbai investment banker, created the app Break Free to curb compulsive usage. He explains:

> *Social media is embedded in my generation. We're wired to crave connection, and every like releases dopamine, reinforcing addiction. During COVID, I realized I was obsessing over strangers' lives instead of nurturing real friendships. My app introduces 'friction' to break mindless scrolling habits.*
>
> *But a blanket ban isn't practical. Social media fuels creativity, business and connections. The solution is education—teaching teens to limit use, cultivate offline interests and model healthy habits.*

Until governments act, digital literacy is key. We'll explore this later. Next, let's examine another threat: the accessibility of online porn to teens.

Online Porn

Online pornography, or the portrayal of sexual subject matter for the purpose of sexual arousal, has become widespread and easily accessible because of smartphones. Studies show (unsurprisingly) that exposure to pornography use in teens can lead to high-risk sexual behaviour and substance use.[23] Teens are exposed to pornography more frequently both intentionally and unintentionally due to a variety of factors, including the normal development of sexuality that peaks during adolescence and because they are naturally curious about sex. Also, we parents are rather ineffective at communicating with our children about all this. Add to this a lack of formal sex education and our teens become even more vulnerable to the ill effects of pornographic content. Pornographic content can seem realistic to a young adolescent which is problematic in many ways.

Porn videos show men and women with enhanced bodies and this affects a teens perception about their own body, appearance and/or sexual performance. Further, the pervasiveness of harmful gender stereotypes and men's violence against women increases the risk of intimate partner violence.[24] Finally, as stated earlier, researchers have observed that the rise in new technologies is making it easier for vulnerable teens to use pornography compulsively and get addicted.[25]

Dr Fiona Miranda is a sexual health educator with over two decades of experience. She had this to share:[26]

> *Porn is our teens' first sex education. Because of taboos that we have created in society, our conditioning is such that we adults believe that we can't talk about sexual development and our teens are too afraid to ask us out of fear of being judged by us. Being judged by their parents is the last thing they want. As our teens have nowhere to access this information, they turn to the wrong place—porn—which is so easily available. Once they access porn, their whole perspective about sex can and often does change. They can develop an unrealistic and a misogynistic view where women are objectified and not on an equal platform. A view that female pleasure is not important, that emotions aren't involved and that commitment isn't required. Also, safe sex isn't depicted in pornographic content and all of these things can have a massive impact on both mental and physical health.*
>
> *How it can affect teens' mentally is that when they watch porn they don't realize that they aren't supposed to look like that. They don't know that everyone grows at their own pace. I know of girls whose self-esteem has suffered after being exposed to porn and then they look for other ways to fit in, and they start taking drugs or drinking alcohol. All because they didn't have an adult*

to talk things through with. I have known of young adult men who have caught STDs because of watching too much porn. Why? Because their partner can't satisfy them as they can only orgasm when they watch porn. And they end up experimenting with other partners without thinking of safe sex and end up catching an STD. Today's hookup culture doesn't help where the thinking is if this isn't working, let me try someone else.

The good news is that parents can play a really important role here. I believe it is their duty to set aside their embarrassment and awkwardness by putting the mental and physical health of their child first. Our teens are open to listening to what you have to say and will ask you questions if you are open and non-judgemental about it. One way to respond to their question is: 'Interesting question; where did you learn that word or learn about that?' When they know that they can comfortably come to you with questions, they won't seek that information elsewhere. Both positive and negative content on sex is available online and a good website that parents can go to access responsible information is the family planning association (FPA) website.'

Dr Fiona Miranda's Tips on How to Talk About Sex with Your Teen:

1. Catch the Moment
    - Life's full of natural openings—use them!
    - A pregnancy announcement (family, friend, neighbor)

- TV/movies/songs about love, dating, or LGBTQ+ topics
- Unrealistic body standards (photoshopped ads, celeb pics)
- News stories involving sex or relationships

2. **Ask, Don't Lecture**

   Start with:

   'What do you think about . . .?'

   'What would you do if . . .?'

   'How does this make you feel?'

3. **Listen First**

   Hear them out before correcting myths or adding facts.

4. **Normalize the Awkward**

   If they blush: *'It's okay to feel awkward—this stuff is tricky!'* Reaffirm your values and offer an open-door policy.

5. **Praise Their Courage**

   If they ask you, celebrate! It means they *trust* you.

6. **Stay Neutral**

   Don't assume why they're asking. Try:

   'What have you heard about that?'

   'Tell me what you already know.'

7. **Keep It Simple**

   Short answers win. Define new terms.

8. **Keep the Door Open**

   After answering:

   'What else do you wonder about?'

   'What's going on that made you think of this?'

9. **Check In**

   'Did that answer your question?' or *'What do you think?'*

10. **Google Together**

    If you're stuck: *'Great question! Let's find out.'*

11. **Lose the Judgement**

    Keep your tone curious, not critical—even if their info is off.

12. **Embrace the Cringe**

    Awkwardness is normal. Push through—it gets easier!

The Bottom Line: Talk early. Talk often. Make it safe.

Online Video Gaming

The impact of video games on youth remains a topic of ongoing debate. While some experts highlight benefits like fostering friendships and developing problem-solving skills, others warn of potential harms ranging from physical health issues to addiction. Many games require players to tackle complex puzzles, strategize and adapt to challenges—skills that translate to real-world cognitive benefits. Research shows gaming can enhance critical thinking, creativity and adaptability. A Canadian study found medical students with gaming experience learned robotic surgery techniques more easily and therapeutic games have proven effective in treating ADHD.[27] The immediate feedback loops in games help players understand cause-and-effect relationships, refining their problem-solving approaches.

However, excessive gaming carries significant risks. Physically, it's linked to obesity due to sedentary behaviour and increased eating during play—studies suggest gaming may disrupt satiety signals or trigger stress-related eating. Repetitive strain injuries like carpal tunnel syndrome and 'gamer's elbow' are also concerns. Psychologically, heavy gaming correlates with sleep disorders, depression and aggression, though more research is needed to confirm causation. Exposure to violent content may desensitize players, potentially influencing behaviour.

The most severe risk is gaming addiction, officially termed internet gaming disorder (IGD). Cases are rising globally, with teenage boys twice as vulnerable as girls. This addiction mirrors substance dependence, hijacking the brain's reward system through dopamine release. Tragedies like a Pune teen's 2024 suicide—reportedly driven by gaming addition—highlight its dangers.[28] Dr Manoj Sharma of NIMHANS reports treating 15–20 new gaming addiction cases weekly, mostly adolescents, noting a post-pandemic surge.

The key lies in balance. When integrated into a healthy lifestyle—with limits on screen time, emphasis on physical activity and real-world socializing—gaming can be a harmless leisure activity. Parents should encourage diverse interests, open communication and monitor usage to harness gaming's benefits while mitigating its risks.

Digital Resilience: Literacy, Hygiene and Safety

> *'Considering that I grew up without a smartphone, I would say life was happier and simpler then. But change is constant, so we must teach our children to use technology with purpose and moderation—and to exercise their will to choose. Today it's social media; tomorrow it will be generative AI. Regulate*

gadget use from the beginning. Set clear expectations, just as you taught them to use crayons on paper, not walls.'

—Dr Anagha Pandit,
clinical psychologist and therapist,
Child Central Clinic, Bengaluru

Digital resilience begins with understanding that while technology is inevitable, mindful use is essential. As Dr Anagha Pandit observes: 'We must teach children to use technology with purpose and moderation, just as we taught them to use crayons properly.' UNICEF defines digital literacy as 'the knowledge, skills and attitudes that allow children to flourish in a digital world while staying safe and empowered.'[29] Teens today navigate complex online landscapes where critical thinking about content, managing digital footprints and understanding privacy implications are crucial survival skills.

The digital world presents unique challenges to adolescent development. Over half of teens use screens before bedtime, disrupting sleep patterns crucial for brain development. Social media exposes users to hundreds of curated images daily, fostering unrealistic beauty standards. A 2023 American Psychological Association study demonstrated that reducing screen time by just 50 per cent for four weeks significantly improved body image perceptions among teens.[30] As tech entrepreneur Savr Kumar advises: 'Mornings are our most creative time—don't waste them reacting to notifications. Similarly, disconnect at least an hour before bed.'

Parents play a vital role in modelling balanced digital habits. While parental controls help, teens ultimately need to internalize self-regulation skills. Dr. Shuchi Grover, an AI and education researcher, emphasizes: 'Teens understand they're trading privacy for connectivity, so we must help them build positive digital identities that will serve them in college and career applications.' Teaching proper citation methods becomes increasingly important in the age of AI tools like ChatGPT, where the line between research and plagiarism blurs.

Ultimately, digital resilience combines literacy, hygiene and safety. It's about empowering teens to harness technology's benefits while developing the wisdom to navigate its pitfalls—whether in gaming, social media or emerging platforms. By fostering open dialogue, setting clear boundaries and encouraging diverse offline interests, we can help young people thrive in our increasingly digital world without being consumed by it.

UNICEF Guidelines for Digital Hygiene and Safety:[31]

1. Teach your teen not to keep their fears to themselves. If they are worried about their safety or something that has happened to them online, they need to urgently speak to you or another adult they trust.
2. Teach them to respect what other people are saying on social media, even if they do not agree with their views.
3. Teach them to respect others, their privacy and their dignity. Teach them that it is not okay to log into other people's accounts or to use their phones or profiles without their permission. Additionally, it is not okay to post/share hurtful or embarrassing stories or photos. What may seem like a harmless joke to one person can be deeply hurtful to others. We all have the right to dignity and to be treated with respect.
4. Teach them to think twice before they click 'send'—especially if they are upset or angry. Once a photo or a video is shared, it's hard to control what happens to it and who sees it. And taking it down is nearly impossible.
5. Tell them that if they see something that is hurtful or offensive, they can report it. On many social media platforms, you can report a specific post or photo if it is against the community standards of the social media platform. Most social media platforms let you 'block'

a person so that you don't see their content and they cannot contact you or send you messages.

6. Show them how to change the privacy settings on their social media platforms to help them control who sees their information, photos and videos. They must learn to think carefully about what they share with whom. It may seem obvious but you still need to tell them not to share personal information like their address, phone number or bank details. If their privacy settings are not secure, anyone can see this information.
7. Tell them not to feel pressured to accept random friend requests. Random people should not be able to see information that you don't want them to see. Tell your teens that sometimes people pretend to be someone they are not, and it's hard to know if they are telling the truth about who they are.
8. Tell them to be careful about any job offers that they receive online. If they didn't apply for a job or contact anyone and someone contacted them, it could be a scam and they need to be very careful. They must do some research about the company or business. Teach them to be careful when going to meet someone for the first time if they have only met them online. They should ask an adult they know well and trust to come with them and arrange to meet in a public place.

We may notice that our teen is using technology excessively. To know what to do in that situation, here are some guidelines:

- Helping teens navigate technology isn't about sudden bans or harsh restrictions—it's about balance, understanding and gradual change.
- Start by having open conversations about mindful tech use rather than confiscating devices outright.
- Prioritize quality family time; connection is the antidote to digital overload.
- Educate them about online risks—cyberbullying, privacy breaches—not to scare them, but to empower them with knowledge.

Criticism and excessive academic pressure often push teens deeper into screens as an escape. Instead, meet them with empathy, not judgment. Small, consistent steps work best: reintroduce real-world routines gently, encourage face-to-face interactions and let genuine relationships naturally displace excessive scrolling. If progress feels slow, don't hesitate to seek professional guidance—but approach the conversation with patience, not threats.

Remember, this is a tightrope walk. Your own habits set the tone. When teens see you practicing digital discipline—putting away your phone during meals, prioritizing presence—they learn by example. Change won't happen overnight, but with steady effort, you'll help them build a healthier relationship with technology and with the world beyond the screen.

Supporting our teens' digital resilience is our responsibility as parents and caregivers. Teaching them about digital literacy, hygiene and safety is as crucial to their well-being—and as fundamental to their success—as their academic education.

Key Takeaways: Chapter 3

1. **The Digital Toll**
   Excessive screen time correlates with increased anxiety, sleep disturbances and diminished academic performance.

2. **The Comparison Trap**
   Social media fosters unrealistic performance pressures that erode authentic self-worth.

3. **The Validation Cycle**
   The pursuit of peer approval online amplifies emotional volatility and risk-taking behaviours.

4. **Parental Leadership**

   Effective digital parenting rbalanced tech use and enforcing developmentally-appropriate boundaries.

5. **Real-World Anchors**

   Prioritize face-to-face connections and teach analytical evaluation of online content.

Genius Bonus Point: The Resilience Reset Button

Create weekly 'digital sunset' rituals where the entire family disconnects to engage in meaningful offline activities—cooking together, stargazing or storytelling. These intentional breaks rebuild attention spans while strengthening emotional bonds that no algorithm can replicate.

4

Resilient Parenting

Showing Up for Your Teen, Showing Up for Yourself

'It's not only children who grow. Parents do too. As much as we watch to see what our children do with their lives, they are watching us to see what we do with ours.'

—Joyce Maynard

Stephen Mc Gowan is a South African banker based in London who was held captive by Mali-based Al-Qaeda group for six years and finally released in July 2017. He was kidnapped by the group from the tourist town of Timbuktu while on a motorcycle tour of Africa. We met in Bengaluru in 2023 and I was struck by his sunny disposition. There was no bitterness that one would imagine would creep in after such a harrowing experience. I asked him about how he had managed to stay positive through the ordeal; what was his secret of resilience. He attributed it to the way he was raised by his parents and shared his thoughts:

My father was always light-hearted, with a warm, driven 'never give up' attitude. He would see the best in everything. My mother was friendly, empathetic, loving and had a million friends who appreciated her warmth and honesty. My mother put relationships first and was the centre of every gathering. My parents' guidance played out by them encouraging me to try different sports. I was never the best but they always supported me and were proud. They created an environment for me to stand on my own two feet, empowered, excited and passionate for the future, not fearful. They also taught me not to take life too seriously.

I believe that the values which I learnt from my parents were the reason for me being released, having grown as a person and not coming out traumatized from the kidnapping. Obviously, growth is not one-sided. We can be taught well, but if you choose not to learn it is our own fault. We all get one life, and because of this I think teenagers must learn the importance of embracing life and striving to be the best version of themselves.

Life is about people! I realized in captivity that my fancy expensive schooling did not make me better than anybody else. I realized the importance of being grateful every day and appreciating the small things in life. I realized that I needed to focus on people if I was going to survive. I realized that I must not be judgemental but rather embrace other people's opinions, cultures and thoughts. I do not necessarily have to agree with their ideas, but the human connection and excitement in different cultures and ideas is the cement that keeps us together. Finally, I learnt the importance of being gentle with people and the power of a friendly smile.

Stephen's story is incredible and inspiring. While none of us would wish for our children to endure what he did, if they had to face such a trial, we would all hope for them to return to their families as he did.

Parenting teenagers marks a shift—the physically exhausting early years may be behind us, but the mental and emotional demands intensify. As our children enter adolescence, many of us are navigating middle age, bringing its own challenges: concerns about health, longevity, marital stability, and, for those with aging parents, the added responsibility of managing their care.

For women, this phase often coincides with menopause, which can range from mild discomfort to debilitating symptoms—anxiety, joint pain, night sweats—further complicating an already demanding stage of life.

Megha Sekhsaria Mawandia, a trained counselor and founder of Triyoke: Raising Parents (a nonprofit providing mental health and parenting support), shared valuable insights from her years of working with parents and teens. Her perspective helped refine my own parenting approach. Here's what she had to say:

> *By the time children become teenagers and young adults, their parents have been married for fifteen to twenty years. Often these parents are feeling unsupported by each other. They are also at a point in their lives when their own parents are aging,*

leading to the emotional and financial stresses that are part of caregiving for ageing parents. While the village (extended community of friends and family) shows up when the children are young, the village disappears when these same children become teenagers. And parents are simply exhausted—they just don't have enough juice to give.

It also doesn't help that teenagers no longer look like the cute cherubic children they once were. This can be triggering for some parents who haven't resolved their childhood traumas. Patterns from the parents' childhood can show up and play out in damaging ways. For example, in a relationship between a mother and a son, the experience of rejection from a son can remind her of her experience with her father and her brothers. And if it's a daughter, the mother could respond with the attitude that I didn't get any kindness from my mother so why should I give it to you.

It would help tremendously if parents were to recognize that they are struggling and that marriages are hard during this phase of life. If they would talk openly, it would help. In my practice, I find that just my acknowledgement that it's been a hard and tiring journey for my client parents makes them feel seen and gives them a burst of energy.

Parents need to think of raising teens as a team sport. Parenting teens gets easier when you work together while being supportive of each other. And when the lines of communication between the spouses are open, this gives you a safe space to vent about your teen without inhibition. Venting to people outside the family unit can backfire because our teens can get judged harshly for their actions. Teenage years are experimental years where we aren't going to see the values we taught them shining through all the time, so talking about your teens' transgressions with those outside the family unit isn't helpful. And your teen needs you to respect their privacy and will not want you discussing their mistakes. If you were to put yourself in their shoes, you wouldn't want that either!

Parenting is one of the world's hardest jobs—and one we're never formally trained for. Yet if adapting our behaviour can support our children's mental well-being, that effort is non-negotiable. Our teens deserve a relationship where they feel safe, secure, and valued—a haven from the outside world. Unconditional love and respect must go hand in hand.

Active listening is key. When engaging with your teen, be present, empathetic, and open-minded—even when you disagree. Respecting their perspectives (however different from yours) fosters mutual understanding. This "mirror effect" encourages them to reciprocate, valuing your views in return. True listening eases loneliness and anxiety; dismissing their concerns risks leaving them feeling hurt, defensive, or unheard. A simple rule? Put your phone away during conversations.

The foundation lies in nurturing the bond you built in their early years. Here are evidence-backed strategies (from UNICEF and WHO) to strengthen your relationship with your teen,[1]

Ten Tips For Improving Your Communication With Your Teen

1. **Show Interest in Their Life**

   Ask questions about what matters to your teen—whether it's a sport they play, a TV show they watch or a hobby they're involved in. Follow up after events, such as matches or performances, to show your support.

2. **Share Your Own Experiences**

   Connect by sharing stories from your life and discovering common interests. You might be surprised to find you have more in common with your often-sullen teen than you thought.

3. **Seek Their Views and Opinions**

   Ask your teen about their perspectives on current events. This demonstrates respect for their thoughts and helps clarify their values.

4. **Pay Attention with Body Language**

   Maintain eye contact, nod occasionally, smile encouragingly—your natural body language communicates interest and care without words. It shows your teen that you're genuinely listening.

5. **Ask Open-Ended, Clarifying Questions**
   Use questions like, *'Can you explain what you meant when you said . . .?'* or *'What was going through your mind when . . .?'* Activities like cooking, driving or walking is often an ideal time to encourage deeper conversations and gain insights into their thoughts and feelings.

6. **Reflect and Mirror Their Words**
   Paraphrase what your teen says to help them feel understood and to clarify their own thoughts.

7. **Give Positive Feedback and Affirmation**
   Provide specific, immediate praise to boost their confidence. For example, *'Thank you for sharing how you're feeling—that's really brave of you.'*

8. **Validate Their Feelings**
   Acknowledge their emotions to help them accept and express them safely. For instance, *'It's understandable you're feeling angry right now. I'd feel the same in your situation.'*

9. **Be Supportive When They're Worrying**
   If your teen finds it hard to talk, let them know you're there for them, ready to listen anytime, without pressing for details.

10. **Share Fun and Positive Moments**
    Communication isn't only about tough topics. Share funny stories, celebrate successes and find opportunities to laugh and be affectionate in ways your teen feels comfortable. These moments strengthen your bond and foster a positive relationship.

Our best efforts at keeping the lines of communication open can still be fraught with challenges. One Bengaluru-based journalist, a mother of two daughters, shared her experience candidly: 'A big learning for me has been that in an effort to treat my daughters fairly, I communicated with them in exactly the same way. Now that they are adults, I know that this was a mistake.'

She had since had honest conversations with her older daughter—now a flourishing young adult—about how certain parenting approaches and words used in her upbringing weren't always helpful and were sometimes downright hurtful. This realization came as a surprise to the journalist: 'My younger daughter and I would have verbal smackdowns quite often but somehow and despite the harsh things that were said by us both, we would forget the terrible things said and often come away with a positive takeaway that was useful to both of us going forward.'

Her older daughter couldn't handle confrontation the same way that her younger daughter could. The good news is that because parenting is a lifelong relationship, there is always time to course correct as long as the lines of communication are kept open and there is mutual respect. The journalist signed off with this: 'I think it's okay that if our teens lash out at us every once in a while, for who else can be their safe harbour if not their parents? As long as it's in moderation, it all works itself out, and I find that our teens will find the resources to handle it as they navigate adulthood.'

Most teens navigate adolescence successfully, but those with genetic vulnerabilities to mental health challenges need our support. While recognizing warning signs is crucial, it's often surprisingly difficult to spot them. The consequences of missing these signs can be severe - when mental health issues go undiagnosed in the teenage years, delayed treatment can complicate the illness and make recovery more challenging.

Recognizing Mental Health Issues in Our Teens

Parents are usually the last to know when their teen is struggling. Teens frequently hide their distress and rarely initiate conversations about their problems. Compounding this, parents often struggle to accept that their child might be facing mental health challenges. The reality is these issues have always existed among teens and their prevalence continues to rise. The most common problems include anxiety disorders, mood disturbances, attention deficits, behavioural issues, and increasingly, eating disorders and body dysmorphia.[2]

Subtle changes often provide the first clues—withdrawing from friends and activities, shifts in eating or sleeping patterns, uncharacteristic mood swings or new behavioural problems at school. These signs demand our attention because half of all serious adult psychiatric conditions begin by age fourteen, yet treatment typically doesn't begin until years later. This dangerous gap can lead to a lifetime of consequences. Research shows untreated mental health issues in teens are linked to academic and career struggles, unstable relationships and the potential for conditions to become more severe and treatment-resistant over time.[3] Most tragically, proper treatment could prevent many cases of teen suicide.[4]

There is hopeful news though. Today's treatment options are more effective than ever. Most teens respond remarkably well to talk therapy, and when medication is needed, modern psychiatric drugs offer relief with minimal side effects.[5] These medications are carefully prescribed for the shortest necessary duration and tapered under professional supervision when appropriate.

If you notice concerning changes in your teen, start by consulting your paediatrician who can recommend qualified mental health professionals. Trust your instincts throughout this process—if a therapist doesn't feel right for your family, or if your teen expresses discomfort, continue your search. The right professional should be someone your child feels comfortable opening up to. For more serious cases affecting relationships, schoolwork or basic self-care, seek out a therapist with at least a master's degree in clinical psychology and specific experience working with adolescents.

Remember that therapy isn't only for crises. Even milder struggles or family tensions can benefit from professional support, often resolving more quickly with guidance. The most important thing is to stay attentive, trust your parental instincts and take action when something doesn't seem right. With proper support and timely intervention, teens can overcome these challenges and thrive.

Dr Anagha Pandit, clinical psychologist and therapist, Child Central Clinic, Bengaluru, shared a case study that illustrates this point:

> *There was this child who was about twelve, and her parents had mutually consented to a divorce. She was angry about the*

divorce. She was a very creative child who wrote very well. As part of her therapy, we created stories together to help her bring this emotion, this anger out. Her sadness and frustration were coming out as aggression towards her mother, who, as a single parent, was having trouble handling her. The child had no mental health diagnosis, but her anger was impacting the single most important relationship in her life. In just six sessions, she was able to channelize her emotions in a much better way, her anger management was better and the relationship was improved.

Dr Anagha emphasizes that patience is essential when beginning therapy with your teen. Progress rarely follows a straight path—it may feel painfully slow at first, then show sudden breakthroughs, or conversely, begin with rapid improvements before reaching a plateau. If medication is recommended after psychiatric evaluation, it's important to take this seriously despite potential side effects. The key is to move forward one step at a time, trusting the process while remaining attentive to your teen's needs. She further shares:

I was working with a teenage girl who I felt needed psychiatric evaluation and medication, but her parents were hesitant to take that step of seeing a psychiatrist. The delay led to her going downhill overnight. We had been working together for six months and suddenly she stopped attending sessions even if they were online; she even refused to leave her room. I had to make home visits to re-open the channels of communication.

It's wise to pursue a psychiatric evaluation if your psychologist recommends it. Should medication be prescribed, ask the psychiatrist key questions: Are there side effects to watch for? When might we see improvement? If possible—though I recognize this isn't always feasible—seek a second opinion to confirm both the diagnosis and the treatment plan. For teens facing serious emotional or behavioural challenges, medication can be life-saving; this isn't a decision to take lightly.

As children enter adolescence, we often attribute their behaviour to typical teenage struggles. While this may be partly true, their distress—expressed through behaviour—is real. Parents must stay attentive. Consider this mother's account of her daughter's mental health journey during the transition from middle to high school, which underscores the importance of keeping our eyes, ears, and hearts open.

Lavanya* (name changed) was a quiet, introverted child who spent middle school reading alone in her room. Her mother Meena* (name changed)—an extroverted, straightforward woman—prided herself on understanding her daughter well. 'I always felt like a smart mother, even cocky about parenting,' Meena admitted. 'Everything seemed fine until the pandemic hit during Lavanya's eighth grade. Looking back, we missed the signs—but it's hard to see what you're not looking for, especially when your child's personality differs from yours.'

Meena, mistaking Lavanya's introversion for simple preference for solitude, gave her increasing alone time. The first red flag emerged when Lavanya lost her voice for days during eighth-grade finals due to a panic attack. When her voice returned, Lavanya confessed: 'I've been struggling and felt no one was there for me—not even you.' Shocked, Meena suggested therapy, but Lavanya refused. As things temporarily stabilized, Meena assumed it was an isolated incident.

Ninth grade brought in-person school's return—and frequent panic attacks. Lavanya would melt down en route to school, sometimes requiring Meena to calm her at the gates. 'She found online school easier,' Meena noted—a sentiment echoed by many teens therapists interviewed. After two years isolated, students struggled with classroom fatigue and social anxiety.

When Lavanya began hearing voices, her therapist urged psychiatric intervention. Meena noticed a pattern: Lavanya's suffering manifested as lashing out. One evening, after cruel remarks, Meena heard screams upstairs and found Lavanya sobbing in a foetal position. The therapist referred them to a psychiatrist who dismissed concerns ('She seems okay'), but Meena's instincts pushed her to seek another opinion. This doctor diagnosed severe anxiety and depression. By tenth grade's end, Lavanya began medication and therapy.

'It was agonizing,' Meena recalled. 'Knowing she was suffering yet feeling powerless. This wasn't like treating a cold—it demanded patience. I realized I couldn't fix it alone.' She proposed a gap year, prioritizing mental health over grades, but Lavanya—whose academic success anchored her self-esteem—reacted with anger.

'Parents want instant fixes, but our "help" can backfire,' Meena reflected. 'I said "supportive" things that actually harmed. Learning to step back was crucial.' Initially silent about Lavanya's struggles, Meena eventually confided in friends and family. 'Sharing lifted a weight. I discovered many parents faced similar battles—exchanging resources and solidarity. There's no shame in mental health struggles—speaking up brought me support and let me help others.'

Psychiatrists and counsellors consistently emphasize: Teens need nonjudgmental presence alongside parents who seek their own support. Megha Mawandia pinpointed a key barrier: 'Parental worry blocks open communication. Fear drives anger, silence, or punishment—but if these failed with young children, why expect them to work now?'

She also noted parents often project unfulfilled dreams onto teens: 'Ask: Are you parenting from the past or present? Pushing obsolete success blueprints ignores today's realities. I see twenty-somethings returning to India after failed abroad dreams, culturally adrift because parents prepped them for non-existent lives.'

Megha's words evoke the Japanese proverb *Nana korobi, ya oki*—fall seven times, rise eight. Resilience requires letting teens face adversity—yet fearful parenting often prevents this. As Shailaja Jayaraman, a college admissions guide, observed: 'Don't crack the whip on already-motivated kids. Tune in if behaviour shifts—withdrawal or sullenness may signal deeper issues.'

Harvard's Dr Giselle Perez Lougee studies teen resilience: 'Self-efficacy—the belief "I can handle life's challenges"—is foundational. Parents must examine the gap between their intended messages and what teens hear. Doing things for teens sends the message: "You can't do this alone."' Overprotection breeds fragility; allowing struggle fosters problem-solving and grit.

Four key life lessons build resilience:

- Life isn't fair. Coaching teens to respond (not react) to injustice cultivates maturity.
- Failure fuels growth. Normalizing setbacks as learning opportunities builds persistence.

- No one excels at everything. Accepting limitations teaches humility and teamwork.
- Life is hard—and that's necessary. Shielding teens from stress robs them of self-efficacy.

As Megha summarized: 'Teens must fail to grow. When parents make failure costly, they undermine resilience. Knowing they can rise after falling is what prepares them for life.'[6]

Below are some more parenting tips for helping teens build resilience, adapted from Amy Morin's *13 Things Mentally Strong Parents Don't Do: Raising Self-Assured Children and Training Their Brains for a Life of Happiness, Meaning, and Success* (2017). I found them very useful and I think you will too![7]

Ten Don'ts of Resilient Parenting

1. **Don't Condone a Victim Mentality**
   Getting cut from the soccer team or failing a class doesn't make our teen a victim. Rejection, failure and unfairness are part of life. Rather than allow teens to host pity parties or exaggerate their misfortune, we need to encourage them to turn their struggles into strength.

2. **Don't Parent Out of Guilt**

   We need to learn to tolerate guilt. Guilty feelings lead to unhealthy parenting strategies—like giving in to our teen after saying no.

3. **Don't Make Your Teen the Centre of Your Universe**

   This is tempting, I know! Believe me, I've succumbed to this too, but I stopped when I realized I didn't want my child growing up self-absorbed and entitled. We must teach them to focus on what they have to offer the world, rather than what they're owed.

4. **Don't Allow Fear to Dictate What You Allow Your Teen to Experience**

   Keeping teens inside a protective bubble stunts their development—even if it spares us anxiety. Letting them experience life within sensible boundaries helps build self-efficacy.

5. **Don't Expect Perfection**

   High expectations are healthy, but expecting too much will backfire. We must recognize that teens won't excel at everything. Helping them become the best versions of themselves is the goal.

6. **Don't Let Your Teen Avoid Responsibility**
   Assign age-appropriate duties at home. Expect them to pitch in and learn the skills they need to become responsible citizens.

7. **Don't Shield Your Teen from Pain**
   Teens need firsthand experience tolerating discomfort. Provide support so they gain confidence in handling life's hardships.

8. **Don't Confuse Discipline with Punishment**
   Punishment makes teens suffer for wrongdoing. Discipline teaches them to do better. Our goal is to help them develop self-discipline.

9. **Don't Take Shortcuts to Avoid Discomfort**
   Giving in when teens complain or doing their chores for them is easy—but it teaches unhealthy habits. Hold your ground; they'll thank you later.

10. **Don't Lose Sight of Your Values**
    In today's fast-paced world, it's easy to get caught up in daily tasks. We must keep our values front and centre, ensuring our family lives by them.

Self-Care for Parents

Raising teens is challenging and it's crucial we don't neglect our own well-being. Parenting, especially if our teen struggles with mental health, can leave us overwhelmed or burned out. Self-care isn't selfish—it's essential for maintaining physical, emotional, and mental health.

You can't pour from an empty cup. To be the best parent, you must take care of yourself. Neglecting self-care leads to burnout and strained relationships. Prioritizing it models healthy behaviour for teens, teaching them stress management.

Meeting Your Physical Needs:

- Exercise—yoga, weight training or walking daily.
- Sleep well—prioritize rest and naps when possible.
- Eat right—reduce sugar and processed foods; add fruits, vegetables and healthy fats.
- Massages—regularly, if possible.
- Physical affection—cuddle, kiss or spend quality time with your spouse.
- Relaxing showers/baths—unwind before bed.
- Morning calm—wake early for peaceful alone time.
- Outdoor walks—at least once a week.

Meeting Your Emotional and Social Needs:

- Time with friends—schedule regular social outings.
- Joyful activities—play with a pet, sing or pursue hobbies.
- Creative socializing—adapt gatherings to fit your teen's schedule.
- Laughter—it reduces stress, boosts immunity and improves mood.
- Crying—a natural release; repressing emotions harms health.

Meeting Your Intellectual Needs:

- Keep learning—audiobooks, documentaries or books outside your field.
- Pursue hobbies—like singing, writing or volunteering.
- Write—journaling, blogging or storytelling keeps the mind sharp.
- Volunteer—it stimulates the brain and fosters purpose.

The Power of Self-Compassion

Research shows that self-compassionate parenting reduces anxiety and depression in teens. A Radboud University study found that parents who were less self-critical had teens with fewer mental health struggles.

Ria Patel, a psychology graduate, shares:

> *As a teenager, I questioned my parents' rules. Their guidance didn't always make sense, but they trusted me, creating respect. I didn't want to disappoint them. Now, I see they were protecting me in ways I couldn't grasp then. To parents: your care leaves a lasting impact. Teens may not understand now, but they will.*

Parenting today is more intensive than ever. A University of California study found parents now spend twice as much time on childcare as in the 1960s. With less time and more pressure, self-compassion is crucial.

Be gentle with yourself. All teens have resilience within them—our job is to nurture it.

Key Takeaways: Chapter 4

1. Mirror Effect
   Teens develop resilience by observing it—parental well-being isn't selfish, it's strategic.

2. The Struggle Paradox
   Helicopter parenting deprives teens of the very challenges that build resilience muscles.

3. **Communication Alchemy**
   Non-judgmental listening transforms parent-teen dynamics from transactional to transformational.

4. **Emotional First Aid**
   Validation before solution—presence is more powerful than problem-solving.

5. **Embodied Leadership**
   Your lived habits of emotional regulation and self-care speak louder than parenting lectures.

Genius Bonus Point: The Resilience Ripple Effect

Implement weekly 'Failure Debriefs' where family members share struggles and lessons learned. Parents go first—model vulnerability by discussing your own mistakes at work or in relationships. This ritual:

- Normalizes struggle as part of growth
- Rewires the brain to see failures as data
- Creates neural pathways for resilience
- Builds emotional intimacy through shared vulnerability
- Demonstrates that even adults are works-in-progress

This transforms your home into a resilience incubator where challenges become connection points rather than sources of shame. The most powerful resilience lessons happen in these unscripted moments of authentic human experience.

Epilogue

If I had to choose one word to describe what parenting has meant to me, it would be 'joy'. Pure joy. This doesn't mean every moment is filled with laughter or elation, but witnessing my children—as well as myself and my husband—growing through challenging moments fills me with a sense of marvel. We are explorers in uncharted territory as each child is so uniquely different. We have no visibility into who they are or who they will become. We only have our aspirations and dreams, and from there, we embark on this exploration. We learn, adapt and sometimes change course.

It's important to pause and take in the journey, to celebrate the moments with joy and gratitude, instead of getting lost in the 'must-dos'. Parenting is not a job; it's life. It's joy—if we trust ourselves, our kids and the community of family, friends and educators around us.

In an interview, Divya Balagopal, senior partner at Mundkur Law Partners and parent of three teens, said: 'Lean in and breathe . . .'

Divya's words resonated deeply with me and realigned my thinking. 'Parenting isn't a job, it's life.' And life, I realized, needs a village to sustain itself. We can't do everything alone—and we shouldn't have to. Raising resilient teens also requires support from schools and the extended community.

A study on mental health by the WHO found that schools and communities are some of the most influential social settings in promoting young people's mental health and well-being. Given the rising mental health concerns among teens, schools have a vital role to play. Research supports this—a review of over forty-five studies shows a clear link between the school 'climate' and teen mental health and resilience. The school climate encompasses the physical and social environment, including how safe students feel. Unsurprisingly, studies indicate that teens attending schools with higher levels of bullying are more likely to experience poor mental health. A large US national longitudinal study of adolescent health also found that school climate influences symptoms of depression among teens.

Schools are not only places where mental health can deteriorate but also powerful settings for delivering effective interventions. They can serve as resilient, supportive environments that help prevent mental health problems before they start. Since teens spend most of their waking hours at school, there's growing evidence that school-level interventions can bolster resilience and functioning. It all comes down to leadership and commitment.

Research consistently shows that loneliness and mental health issues often go hand in hand in teens. Loneliness exacerbates depression and anxiety, making community-level interventions crucial. Opportunities for teens to volunteer locally, join sports teams or simply play table tennis with friends can make a significant difference. These activities must be accessible to all.

Resilient teens are more likely to grow into resilient adults—a goal worth striving for.

Thank you for reading.

A Letter to Fellow Parents

Dear Parent,

To raise a child in today's world is to stand in quiet opposition to it.

You are not merely feeding, clothing and schooling a teenager. You are shaping a mind that must stay clear in a fog of half-truths, a heart that must remain soft in a culture that rewards hardness and a body that must endure both pressure and pace. It is a task as ordinary as it is radical.

Let us speak plainly. There is no manual. No formula. No perfect parent. There are only people—tired, worried, hopeful—doing their best each day to raise someone who will survive with integrity and, perhaps, offer some to the world.

What you are doing matters. Quietly refusing the cult of perfection. Turning away from performance parenting. Choosing conversation over commands. This is not weakness—it is moral courage. And it leaves marks that no certificate ever could.

You cannot shield your child from the world. But you can prepare them to meet it without losing themselves. You can teach by example: how to suffer without bitterness, how to fail without collapse, how to think when everyone is shouting.

Parenting is not a series of grand gestures. It is the daily work of presence. Of showing up even when ignored. Of setting limits without anger. Of offering safety without condition. This is not easy. But it is enough.

In the end, your child will not remember all that you said. But they will remember the ground they stood on—and whether it held steady when they could not.

Hold the line. You are not alone.

Warmest regards,
Sujata Kelkar Shetty.

The Blossoming of Teen Resilience

A Final Word

Resilience in adolescence is not a return to wholeness after breaking—it is the luminous transformation that occurs *while* breaking. Imagine a star being born: that cataclysmic collapse of cosmic dust, the violent friction of elements colliding, until suddenly—light. This is the teenager's journey: not bouncing back, but bursting forward through the very pressures meant to crush them.

And yet, too many parents are raising children in cages of perfection. They force endless hours of study, relentless drills, the ceaseless pursuit of external validation. And then, when these children finally step into the real world, they shatter. Because the world does not reward rote memorization or mechanical skill—it rewards *thinking*. It demands resilience, creativity, the ability to adapt and breathe and *play*.

Today's teens exist in a paradox only poets and neuroscientists could fully appreciate. They are the most connected generation in history, yet too often their loneliness echoes like an empty cathedral. They hunger for autonomy with prefrontal cortices still under construction—like master painters given a brush but not yet the full spectrum of colours. Their resilience is not armour, but aliveness: the raw, trembling courage to feel everything and keep choosing life anyway. It whispers in the midnight journal entry smudged with tears, in the shaky hand reaching for a phone to text *'I need help'*, in the defiant act of sitting alone at lunch rather than betraying oneself for belonging.

Science and soul agree: resilience flowers in the interplay of three sacred elements.

- Sanctuary—the safe harbour of one adult who says, *'You are not too much'*.
- Initiation—the necessary trials that carve wisdom into young bones.

- Revelation—those electrifying moments when a teen discovers their voice can shake mountains.

Watch the guitarist translating panic attacks into lyrics, the kid with a stammer teaching classmates chess, the grieving scholar who starts a mental health club. These are not just survivors; they are alchemists turning pain into power.

But look deeper. Every resilient teen is surrounded by invisible hands holding their universe together: the father who admits his own failures at dinner, the teacher who grades effort over perfection, the ancestral whispers of *'We, too, survived'*. Like mycelium beneath a forest, this interconnected strength nourishes growth unseen.

Do not mistake privilege for invulnerability. Behind every polished uniform and prestigious address, there are boarding school children who weep into their pillows at night—aching with a loneliness no material comfort can soothe. There are those who shrink from their own advantages, stepping out of chauffeur-driven cars blocks from school, weighted by shame no one anticipates.

Comparison is the thief of compassion—for your child, and for others. When you measure your teen against those who seem to *'have it all'*, remember: the greenest grass often grows over the deepest cracks. Every child carries invisible battles; every family has its silent wars. What looks like ease may be exhaustion in disguise and what appears seamless may be barely held together.

To witness teen resilience is to stand before a living masterpiece—one where the cracks are gilded with the gold of hard-won wisdom, where every scar tells the story of a self still choosing to bloom. They are the most breathtaking argument for hope this world has: not because they are unbreakable, but because they keep finding new ways to shine through the broken places.

Here lies the secret adults so often forget: teens don't need to be fixed or turned into drones. They need to be seen—in their glorious, messy becoming—and reminded: *Your light is not despite the cracks, but because of them.*

No one is perfect. No system is flawless. But if we sacrifice our children's joy, their curiosity, their very humanity at the altar of achievement, what have we truly gained?

Perhaps these words belong nowhere. Or perhaps they are the quiet heartbeat of this book—a reminder that education without breath is just another kind of suffocation.

Good luck growing resilience in your beloved teens!

Teen Brain Upgrade Checklist

Feed it (omega-3s), move it (exercise), rest it (nine hours sleep), challenge it (learn new skills).

1. Fuel It Right
   - Eat brain foods: Omega-3s (fish, nuts), antioxidants (berries) and iron (spinach).
   - Ditch sugar crashes—swap junk for nuts, fruits, dark chocolate.

2. Move It Daily
   - Sixty mins of *anything*: Dance, sports, yoga, even walking.

Bonus: Exercise = instant mood boost.

3. Sleep Like a Boss
    - Nine hours/night. No screens one hour before bed.

      Pro tip: Sleep = memory upgrade.

4. Challenge It
    - Learn something new (language, instrument, coding).
    - Solve puzzles, read, debate—flex that brain muscle.

5. Pause & Reset
    - Five-minute mindfulness or deep breathing when stressed.
    - Journaling = emotional decluttering.

6. Connect IRL
    - Face-to-face over screens. Laugh with friends, hug family.
    - Loneliness = brain drain.

7. Protect It
    - Social media detox one day/week.
    - Say no to doomscrolling—your focus is precious.

Parent-Teen Resilience Check-In Questionnaire

Share one answer with your teen tonight—and LISTEN to theirs.

Section 1: Understanding Your Teen

1. On a scale of 1–10, how would you rate your teen's current stress level? What's driving it?
2. What's one thing your teen does that surprises you with their resilience?
3. What's their go-to coping mechanism when upset (e.g., music, isolation, talking)?

Section 2: Habits & Environment

4. Does your teen get 8–9 hours of sleep regularly? If not, what's the biggest barrier?
5. What's one small change you could make at home to support their mental fuel (nutrition, downtime, etc.)?
6. How does your family *model* resilience (e.g., handling setbacks, self-care)?

Section 3: Digital World

7. What's your teen's *healthy* tech habit? What's their *riskiest*?
8. Have you talked about online porn/social media pitfalls? What worked (or didn't)?

Section 4: Communication

9. Finish the sentence: 'When my teen shuts down, I usually . . .' (e.g., push, wait, distract).
10. What's one question your teen *wishes* you'd ask them? (Guess, then ask them later!)

Section 5: Growth

11. What's one resilience skill you want to help your teen build this year?
12. What's one you'd like to work on yourself?

Parent Resilience Check-In Quiz

(Self-Assessment for Burnout and Balance)

Rate Yourself (1–5): 1 *'I'm running on fumes'* 5 *'I'm thriving'*

1. Energy Levels
   - *When did you last take a guilt-free break?*
     (1: 'Can't remember' → 5: 'This week!')

2. Stress Signals
   - *How often do you feel irritable/overwhelmed?*
     (1: 'Daily' → 5: 'Rarely')

3. Self-Care
   - *What's your non-negotiable recharge ritual?*
     (1: 'What's that?' → 5: 'Yoga/walks/therapy/etc.')

4. Role Modelling
   - *Do you talk about your struggles openly?*
     (1: 'Never—I hide it' → 5: 'Yes, to show resilience')

5. Support System
   - *Who's your go-to person when you're drained?*
     (1: 'No one' → 5: "I have more than two trusted allies')

Reflection Questions

- *What's one small step you'll take this week to refuel?*
- *How can you turn your teen's challenges into shared growth?*

Key Insight: Your teen mirrors your stress—and your resilience.

Book Tie-In: Revisit Chapter 4's 'Self-Care Strategies for Parents'.
Note: Scored <10? Prioritize yourself—you can't pour from an empty cup.

Acknowledgements

Writing this book has been a beautiful journey. One that has deepened my commitment to a most fulfilling vocation—motherhood. People came forward to support this book in the most unexpected and lovely ways.

My heartfelt thanks to the talented and energetic young people who shared their stories with me. Your truths gave the book lyrical resonance and helped us oldies understand what it's like to walk in your shoes.

A big thank you to the psychologists, doctors and researchers who took the time to answer my questions. Your words have us valuable advice on how to, and more importantly not to, parent.

Deepthi and the editorial team at Penguin Random House India, I thank you for support and guidance. Jayapriya Vasudevan, thank you for expertly guiding me through the publishing process. Ria Patel, thank you for creating the outline of the book and for making interview notes. This book was that much easier to write knowing that I had all your unwavering support.

My friends from my past and present, thank you for your generous encouragement and enthusiastic support. So many of you told me that this book was the need of the hour. That message kept me going and get to the finish line.

My parents Lata and Vijay Kelkar, thank you for your unwavering love and guidance. You enthusiastically connected me with so many experts who are quoted in the book. Most of all, a million thanks for being the kind of parents who supported me unconditionally and loved me without bounds. It built my resilience.

My dear husband Nitesh, thank you for being my loving anchor. Thank you for being open to learning and change as we navigate parenting our beloved sons together.

My teenagers Akash and Aarav, this book is dedicated to you because without your light in my life I wouldn't have strung a sentence together on the subject, much less written a book about teens.

Notes

Introduction

1 Chavira, D.A., Ponting, C. and Ramos, G., 'The impact of COVID-19 on child and adolescent mental health and treatment considerations' *Behaviour Research and Therapy* 157 (2022), https://doi.org/10.1016/j.brat.2022.104169.

2 Kakollu, S. and Dar, A.A., 'Mental health of young adults pursuing higher education in Tier-1 cities of India: A cross-sectional study', *Asian Journal of Psychiatry* 106 (2025), https://doi.org/10.1016/j.ajp.2025.104447.

3 'Online learning in COVID-19 detrimental to teen mental health, school satisfaction, performance',

ScienceDaily, 30 November 2022, https://www.sciencedaily.com/releases/2022/11/221130151529.htm.

4 Vaidya, R. et al., 'Depression, Anxiety, and Stress among Indian Youth during the COVID-19 Lockdown-A Cross-Sectional Survey', *Journal of Mental Health and Human Behaviour* 26, no. 2 (2021): 153–60, https://doi.org/10.4103/jmhhb.jmhhb_65_21.

5 Collier Villaume, S. et al., 'Age Disparities in Prevalence of Anxiety and Depression Among US Adults During the COVID-19 Pandemic', *JAMA Network Open* 6, no. 11 (2023): e2345073, https://doi.org/10.1001/jamanetworkopen.2023.45073.

6 Vigdal, J.S. and Brønnick, K.K., 'A Systematic Review of "Helicopter Parenting" and Its Relationship With Anxiety and Depression', *Frontiers in Psychology* 13 (2022): 872981, https://doi.org/10.3389/fpsyg.2022.872981.

Chapter 1: The Ferrari Brain

1 'Teenage Brain: A Work in Progress', National Institute of Mental Health Fact Sheet, 2001, https://www.nimh.nih.gov/health/publications/teenage-brain-a-work-in-progress.

2 Lenroot, R.K. and Giedd, J.N., 'Brain development in children and adolescents: Insights from anatomical magnetic resonance imaging' *Neuroscience*

and Biobehavioral Reviews 30, no. 6 (2006), https://doi.org/10.1016/j.neubiorev.2006.06.001.

3 Allstate Insurance Company and Sperling's BestPlaces, 'America's Teen Driving Hotspots Study', May 2008.

4 SaveLIFE Foundation, https://savelifefoundation.org.

5 Naveh-Benjamin, M., Kilb, A. and Fisher, T., 'Concurrent task effects on memory encoding and retrieval: further support for an asymmetry', *Memory and Cognition* 34, no. 1, January 2006, doi: 10.3758/bf03193389. PMID: 16686109.

6 Talevski, J. et. al., 'Teach-Back: A Systematic Review of Implementation and Impacts', *PLOS ONE 15*(4), 2020, https://doi.org/10.1371/journal.pone.0231350.

7 Kilroy, E. et al., 'Relationships Between Cerebral Blood Flow and IQ in Typically Developing Children and Adolescents', *Journal of Cognitive Science* 12, no, 2011, https://doi.org/10.17791/jcs.2011.12.2.151.

8 Kuhn, D., 'Adolescent Thinking', in *Handbook of Adolescent Psychology*, 3rd ed., vol. 1, ed. R.M. Lerner and L. Steinberg (Hoboken, NJ: John Wiley & Sons, 2009), 152–86.

9 Larson, R. and Rusk, N., 'Intrinsic Motivation and Positive Development', in *Advances in Child Development and Behavior: Positive Youth Development*, ed. R. Lerner (Oxford: Elsevier, 2011).

10 Seligman, C.K. and Rider, E.A., *Life Span Human Development*, 7th ed. (Belmont, CA: Wadsworth Publishing, 2012).

11 Ramsden, S. et al., 2011, 'Verbal and non-verbal intelligence changes in the teenage brain', *Nature* 479, https://doi.org/10.1038/nature10514.

12 Ewell, S.N. et al., 'A Comparison of Study Behaviors and Metacognitive Evaluation Used by Biology Students', *CBE—Life Sciences Education* 22, no. 4 (December 2023): ar36, https://doi.org/10.1187/cbe.22-11-0225.

13 Potter, M.C. et al., 'Detecting Meaning in RSVP at 13 ms per Picture', *Attention, Perception, and Psychophysics* 76, no. 2, February 2014 270–79, https://doi.org/10.3758/s13414-013-0605-z.

14 Karpicke, J.D. and Bauernschmidt, A., 'Spaced Retrieval: Absolute Spacing Enhances Learning Regardless of Relative Spacing', *Journal of Experimental Psychology: Learning, Memory, and Cognition* 37, no. 5 (September 2011): 1250–57, https://doi.org/10.1037/a0023436.

15 Ward, A.F. et al., 'Brain Drain: The Mere Presence of One's Own Smartphone Reduces Available Cognitive Capacity', *Journal of the Association for Consumer Research* 2, no. 2, 2017 140–54, https://doi.org/10.1086/691462.

16 Chein, J. et al., 'Peers Increase Adolescent Risk-Taking by Enhancing Activity in the Brain's Reward

Circuitry', *Developmental Science* 14, no. 2 (March 2011): F1–10, https://doi.org/10.1111/j.1467-7687.2010.01035.x.

17 Galván, A., 'Adolescent Development of the Reward System', *Frontiers in Human Neuroscience* 4 (2010): 6, https://doi.org/10.3389/neuro.09.006.2010.

18 Do, K.T., Guassi Moreira, J.F. and Telzer, E.H., 'But Is Helping You Worth the Risk? Defining Prosocial Risk Taking in Adolescence', *Developmental Cognitive Neuroscience* 25 (June 2017): 260–71, https://doi.org/10.1016/j.dcn.2016.11.008.

19 Dahl, R.E., 'Affect Regulation, Brain Development, and Behavioral/Emotional Health in Adolescence', *CNS Spectrums* 6, no. 1 (January 2001): 60–72, https://doi.org/10.1017/s1092852900022884.

20 Payne, M., 'All Gas and No Brakes!: Helpful Metaphor or Harmful Stereotype?', *Journal of Adolescent Research* 27 (2011), https://doi.org/10.1177/0743558411412956.

21 Casey, B. and Caudle, K., 'The Teenage Brain: Self-Control', *Current Directions in Psychological Science* 22, no. 2 (April 2013): pp. 82–87, https://doi.org/10.1177/0963721413480170.

22 Radhakrishnan, R. and Andrade, C., 'Suicide: An Indian Perspective', *Indian Journal of Psychiatry* 54, no. 4 (October 2012): 304–19.

23 Swain, P.K. et al., 'Forecasting Suicide Rates in India: An Empirical Exposition', *PLOS ONE* 16, no. 7 (2021): e0255342.

24 Mueller, A.S. et al., 'The Social Roots of Suicide: Theorizing How the External Social World Matters to Suicide and Suicide Prevention', *Frontiers in Psychology* 12 (2021): 763, https://doi.org/10.3389/fpsyg.2021.621569.

25 Manohar, W.S., Damodar, G. and Sheikh, N.A., 'Microanalysis of the Adolescents Suicides', *Indian Journal of Forensic Medicine and Pathology* 9, no. 2 (2016): 51.

26 Lalwani, S. et al., 'Suicide Among Children and Adolescents in South Delhi (1991–2000)', *Indian Journal of Pediatrics* 71 (2004): 701–03, https://doi.org/10.1007/BF02730657.

27 Arun, P. and Chavan, B., 'Stress and Suicidal Ideas in Adolescent Students in Chandigarh', *Indian Journal of Medical Sciences* 63, no. 7 (2009): 281.

28 Gvion, Y. and Apter, A., 'Aggression, Impulsivity, and Suicide Behaviour: A Review of the Literature', *Archives of Suicide Research* 15 (2011): 93–112.

Chapter 2: Resilience Boosters: Movement, Fuel, Sleep and Creativity

1 Singh, S., 'Bullying Among Indian Schoolgoing Children: A Review', *Education India: A Quarterly Refereed Journal of Dialogues on Education, A UGCCARE List Journal* 11, no. 4 (November 2022), http://www.educationindiajournal.org

2 'Physical inactivity a leading cause of disease and disability, warns WHO', World Health Organization, https://www.who.int/news/item/04-04-2002-physical-inactivitya-leading-cause-of-disease-and-disability-warns-who.

3 Singh, B. et al., 'Effectiveness of Physical Activity Interventions for Improving Depression, Anxiety and Distress: An Overview of Systematic Reviews', *British Journal of Sports Medicine* 57 (2023): 1203–09.

4 'Physical Activity – Fact Sheet', World Health Organization, https://www.who.int/en/news-room/fact-s.

5 Slater, A. and Tiggemann, M., "Uncool to Do Sport': A Focus Group Study of Adolescent Girls' Reasons for Withdrawing from Physical Activity', *Psychology of Sport and Exercise* 11, no. 6 (2010): 619–26, https://doi.org/10.1016/j.psychsport.2010.07.006.

6 Füzéki, E., Groneberg, D.A. and Banzer, W., 'Physical Activity during COVID-19 Induced Lockdown: Recommendations', *Journal of Occupational Medicine and Toxicology* 15 (2020): 25, https://doi.org/10.1186/s12995-020-00278-9.

7 Jeong, Y.-J. et al., 'Dance Movement Therapy Improves Emotional Responses and Modulates Neurohormones in Adolescents with Mild Depression', *International Journal of Neuroscience* 115, no. 12 (2005): 1711–20.

8 Lane, M.M. et al., 'Ultra-Processed Food Consumption and Mental Health: A Systematic Review and Meta-Analysis of Observational Studies', *Nutrients* 14, no. 13 (21 June 2022): 2568.

9 Terry, N. and Margolis, K.G., 'Serotonergic Mechanisms Regulating the Gastrointestinal Tract: Experimental Evidence and Therapeutic Relevance', in *Handbook of Experimental Pharmacology* 239 (2017): 319–42, https://doi.org/10.1007/164_2016_103.

10 Zielińska, M. et al., 'The Mediterranean Diet and the Western Diet in Adolescent Depression—Current Reports', *Nutrients* 14, no. 20 (19 October 2022): 4390, https://doi.org/10.3390/nu14204390.

11 Chaudhary, A., Sudzina, F. and Mikkelsen, B.E., 'Promoting Healthy Eating among Young People—A Review of the Evidence of the Impact of School-Based Interventions', *Nutrients* 12, no. 9 (22 September 2020): 2894, https://doi.org/10.3390/nu12092894.

12 Hamulka, J. et al., 'Effect of an Education Program on Nutrition Knowledge, Attitudes toward Nutrition, Diet Quality, Lifestyle, and Body Composition in Polish Teenagers: The ABC of Healthy Eating Project—Design, Protocol, and Methodology', *Nutrients* 10, no. 10 (5 October 2018): 1439.

13 Kim, Y. and Je, Y., 'Dietary Fibre Intake and Mortality from Cardiovascular Disease and All

Cancers: A Meta-Analysis of Prospective Cohort Studies', *Archives of Cardiovascular Diseases* 109, no. 1 (2016): 39–54.

14 Van Kleef, E., Shimizu, M. and Wansink, B., 'Just a Bite: Considerably Smaller Snack Portions Satisfy Delayed Hunger and Craving', *Food Quality and Preference* 27 (2013): 96–100, https://doi.org/10.1016/j.foodqual.2012.06.008.

15 Graham, M.G. ed., *Sleep Needs, Patterns, and Difficulties of Adolescents: Summary of a Workshop*, National Research Council (US) and Institute of Medicine (US) Forum on Adolescence (Washington, DC: National Academies Press, 2000).

16 Scullin, M.K. et al., 'The Effects of Bedtime Writing on Difficulty Falling Asleep: A Polysomnographic Study Comparing To-Do Lists and Completed Activity Lists', *Journal of Experimental Psychology: General* 147, no. 1 (January 2018): 139–46.

17 Turmel, D. et al., 'Tailored Individual Yoga Practice Improves Sleep Quality, Fatigue, Anxiety, and Depression in Chronic Insomnia Disorder', *BMC Psychiatry* 22, no. 1 (14 April 2022): 267.

18 Wong, S.D. et al., 'Development of the Circadian System in Early Life: Maternal and Environmental Factors', *Journal of Physiological Anthropology* 41, no. 1 (16 May 2022): 22, https://doi.org/10.1186/s40101-022-00294-0.

19 Tang, M. et al., 'Creativity as a Means to Well-Being in Times of COVID-19 Pandemic: Results of a Cross-Cultural Study', *Frontiers in Psychology* 12 (2021).

20 Acar, S. et al., 'Creativity and Well-Being: A Meta-Analysis', *The Journal of Creative Behavior* 55, no. 3 (2020): 738–51.

21 Zhao, R. et al., 'An Updated Evaluation of the Dichotomous Link Between Creativity and Mental Health', *Frontiers in Psychiatry* 12 (2022).

22 Fancourt, D. and Ali, H., 'Differential Use of Emotion Regulation Strategies When Engaging in Artistic Creative Activities Amongst Those with and Without Depression', *Scientific Reports* 9, no. 1 (2019).

23 Kaufman, J.C., 'Creativity and Mental Illness: So Many Studies, So Many Wrong Conclusions', in *Creativity and Innovation: Theory, Research, and Practice*, ed. J.A. Plucker (Waco, TX: Prufrock Press Inc., 2017), 199–204.

24 'Five-Fifty: Creating Creatives', McKinsey & Company, https://www.mckinsey.com/capabilities/peopleand-organizational-performance/our-insights/fivefifty-creating-creatives#.

25 Drago, V. and Heilman, K.M., 'Creativity', in *Encyclopedia of Human Behavior*, 2nd ed., vol. 1, ed. V.S. Ramachandran (London: Academic Press, 2012), 606–17.

26 Vincent, A.S., Decker, B.P. and Mumford, M.D., 'Divergent Thinking, Intelligence, and Expertise: A Test of Alternative Models', *Creativity Research Journal* 14, no. 2 (2002): 163–78.

Chapter 3: The Digital World: Social Media, Online Porn, Online Video Gaming and Digital Citizenship

1 Small, G.W. et al., 'Brain Health Consequences of Digital Technology Use', *Dialogues in Clinical Neuroscience* 22, no. 2 (June 2020): 179–87.
2 "Brain Rot" Named Oxford Word of the Year 2024', Oxford University Press, https://corp.oup.com/news/brain-rot-namedoxford-word-of-the-year-2024/.
3 Pantic, I., 'Online Social Networking and Mental Health', *Cyberpsychology, Behavior, and Social Networking* 17, no. 10 (2014): 652–57.
4 'New Report Finds Teens Feel Addicted to Their Phones, Causing Tension at Home', Common Sense Media, https://www.commonsensemedia.org/press-releases/newreport-finds-teens-feel-addicted-to-their-phonescausing-tension-at-home.
5 Boniel-Nissim et al., *A Focus on Adolescent Social Media Use and Gaming in Europe, Central Asia and Canada: Health Behaviour in School-Aged Children. International Report*

from the 2021/2022 Survey, vol. 6 (Copenhagen: World Health Organization Regional Office for Europe, 2024), CC BY-NC-SA 3.0 IGO.

6 'Social Media Health Warning', *New York Times*, https://www.nytimes.com/2024/06/17/opinion/social-media-health-warning.html.

7 Social Media and Youth Mental Health: The U.S. Surgeon General's Advisory, U.S. Department of Health and Human Services, https://www.hhs.gov/sites/default/files/sg-youthmental-health-social-media-advisory.pdf.

8 Health Advisory on Social Media Use in Adolescence, American Psychological Association, 2023, https://www.apa.org/topics/social-media-internet/health-advisory-adolescent-social-media-use.pdf.

9 Uhls, Y.T., Ellison, N.B. and Subrahmanyam, K., 'Benefits and Costs of Social Media in Adolescence', *Pediatrics* 140, suppl. 2 (2017): S67–S70, https://doi.org/10.1542/peds.2016-1758E.

10 Anderson, M. and Jiang, J., 'Teens' Social Media Habits and Experiences', Pew Research Center: Internet, Science & Tech (United States of America, 2018), https://www.pewresearch.org/internet/2018/11/28/teens-social-media-habits-and-experiences/.

11 'Teens' Social Media Habits and Experiences', Pew Research Center, https://www.pewresearch.org/

internet/2018/11/28/teens-social-media-habits-and-experiences/.

12 Charmaraman, L., Hernandez, J. and Hodes, R., 'Marginalized and Understudied Populations Using Digital Media', in *Handbook of Adolescent Digital Media Use and Mental Health*, ed. J. Nesi, E. Telzer, and M. Prinstein (Cambridge: Cambridge University Press, 2022), 188–214.

13 Vogels, E. and Gelles-Watnick, R., 'Teens and Social Media: Key Findings from Pew Research Center Surveys', Pew Research Center: Internet, Science & Tech (United States of America, 2023), https://www.pewresearch.org/short-reads/2023/04/24/teens-and-social-media-key-findings-from-pew-research-center-surveys/.

14 Evans-Lacko, S. et al., 'The Impact of Digital Interventions on Help-Seeking Behaviour for Mental Health Problems: A Systematic Literature Review', *Current Opinion in Psychiatry* 35, no. 3 (1 May 2022): 207–18.

15 Ybarra, M.L. et al., 'Online Social Support as a Buffer Against Online and Offline Peer and Sexual Victimization Among U.S. LGBT and Non-LGBT Youth', *Child Abuse and Neglect* 39 (2015): 123–36.

16 Mental State of India Report: October 2023, Sapien Labs, https://sapienlabs.org/wp-content/

uploads/2023/11/Mental-State-of-India-Report-October-2023.pdf.

17 Haidt, J., Testimony Before the United States Senate Judiciary Committee, https://www.judiciary.senate.gov/imo/media/doc/Haidt%20Testimony.pdf.

18 Wells, G., Horwitz, J. and Seetharaman, D., 'Facebook Knows Instagram Is Toxic for Teen Girls, Company Documents Show', *Wall Street Journal*, https://www.wsj.com/articles/facebook-knowsinstagram-is-toxic-for-teen-girls-companydocuments-show-11631620739.

19 Braghieri, L., Levy, R. and Makarin, A., 'Social Media and Mental Health', *American Economic Review* 112, no. 11 (2022): 3660–93.

20 Orben, A. et al., 'Windows of Developmental Sensitivity to Social Media', *Nature Communications* 13, no. 1 (2022): 1649.

21 'Why Australia Plans to Ban Social Media for Those Under 16 Years of Age', *New Indian Express*, https://www.newindianexpress.com/xplore/2024/Nov/08/why-australia-plans-to-ban-social-media-for-those-under-16-years-of-age.

22 'Children and Mobile Addiction', LocalCircles, https://www.localcircles.com/a/press/page/children-mobile-addiction.

23 Luder, M.T. et al., 'Associations Between Online Pornography and Sexual Behaviour Among

Adolescents: Myth or Reality?', *Archives of Sexual Behavior* 40 (2011): 1027–35.

24 Vera-Gray, F. et al., 'Sexual Violence as a Sexual Script in Mainstream Online Pornography', *The British Journal of Criminology* 61, no. 5 (2021): 1243–60.

25 De Alarcón, R. et al., 'Online Porn Addiction: What We Know and What We Don't—A Systematic Review', *Journal of Clinical Medicine* 8, no. 1 (2019): 91.

26 Interview with the author.

27 Peñuelas-Calvo, I. et al., 'Video Games for the Assessment and Treatment of Attention-Deficit/Hyperactivity Disorder: A Systematic Review', *European Child and Adolescent Psychiatry* 31, no. 1 (18 January 2022): 5–20.

28 '16-Year-Old Boy Addicted to Online Game Dies by Suicide Near Pune: Cops', NDTV, https://www.ndtv.com/india-news/16-year-old-boy-addicted-to-online-game-dies-by-suicidenear-pune-cops-6217339.

29 Chaput, J.P. et al., 'Video Game Playing Increases Food Intake in Adolescents: A Randomized Crossover Study', *The American Journal of Clinical Nutrition* 93, no. 6 (June 2011): 1196–1203.

30 'A Teacher's Guide to Digital Literacy and Digital Literacy Skills in the Classroom', University of San Diego Division of Professional and Continuing Education, https://pce.sandiego.edu/digital-literacy/.

31 '10 Tips Teens Can Use to Stay Safe Online', United Nations Children's Fund (UNICEF), https://www.unicef.org/armenia/en/stories/10-tips-teens-can-stay-safe-online.

Chapter 4: Resilient Parenting: Showing Up for Your Teen, Showing Up for Yourself

1 World Health Organization and the United Nations Children's Fund (UNICEF), Teacher's Guide to the Magnificent Mei and Friends Comic Series: Mental Health, Brain Health and Substance Use (MSD), https://www.unicef.org/adolescentmentalhealthhub/media/1641/file/Teachers'-Guide-Magnificent-Mei-English.pdf.

2 American College of Obstetricians and Gynecologists, 'Committee Opinion No. 705: Mental Health Disorders in Adolescents', *Obstetrics and Gynecology* 130, no. 1 (July 2017): e32–e41.

3 Kessler, R.C. and Price, R.H., 'Primary Prevention of Secondary Disorders: A Proposal and Agenda', *American Journal of Community Psychology* 21 (1993): 607–33.

4 Meltzer, H.Y. et al., 'Clozapine Treatment for Suicidality in Schizophrenia: International Suicide Prevention Trial (InterSePT)', *Archives of General Psychiatry* 60 (2003): 82–91.

5 Das, J.K. et al., 'Interventions for Adolescent Mental Health: An Overview of Systematic Reviews', *Journal of Adolescent Health* 59, suppl. 4 (October 2016): S49–S60.

6 Carlén, K., Suominen, S. and Augustine, L., 'The Association Between Adolescents' Self-Esteem and Perceived Mental Well-Being in Sweden in Four Years of Follow-Up', *BMC Psychology* 11 (2023): 413.

7 Morin, A., *13 Things Mentally Strong Parents Don't Do: Raising Self-Assured Children and Training Their Brains for a Life of Happiness, Meaning and Success* (New York: HarperCollins, 2017).

Scan QR code to access the
Penguin Random House India website